Snowflakes For Kids

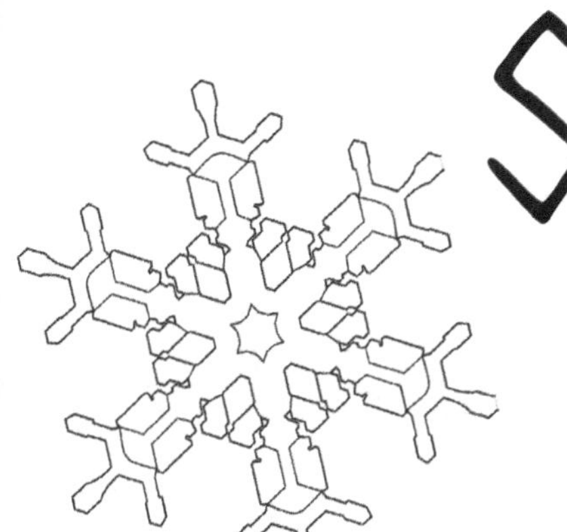

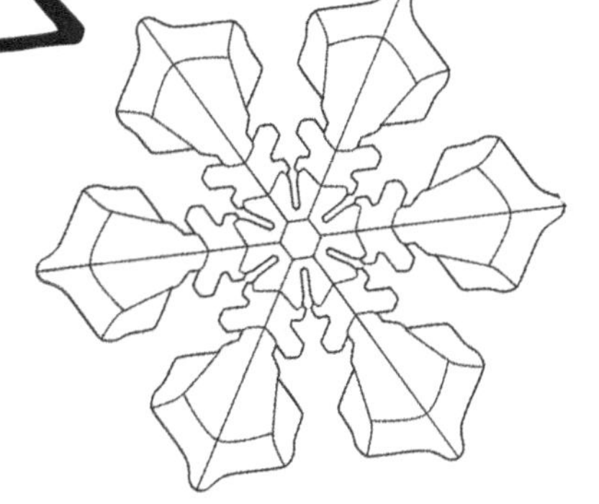

REAL snowflakes for you to color!

Based on photos of actual snowflakes.

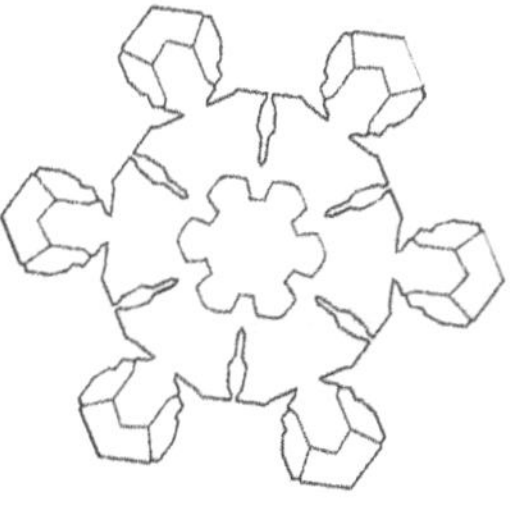

Snowflakes designed by Katie Mullaly

Featuring cover art by Toby Allen

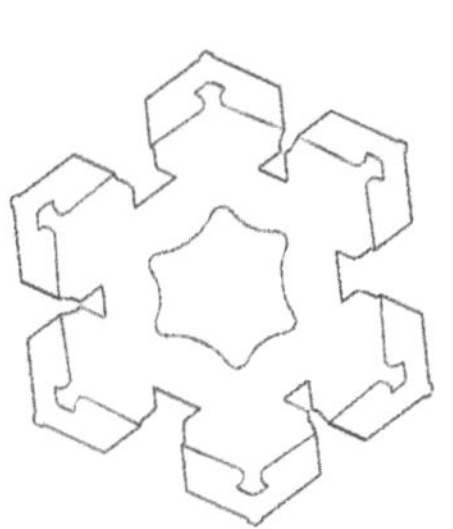

Published by Faceted Press

Copyright © 2016 Faceted Press

ISBN: 978-0-9860997-3-1

www.FacetedPress.com/snowflakes

Snowflakes For Kids

The drawings in this book are based on photos of REAL snowflakes by Kenneth
G. Libbrecht (www.snowcrystals.com) and others.
We took out some of the complicated detail so that your young artists
can feel comfortable coloring them in.

Each one depicts the structure and beauty of a real snowflake for your coloring
fun. So yes, there are snowflakes that actually look like these drawings.

To see images of the real snowflakes that we used for this book
go to www.FacetedPress/snowflakes.

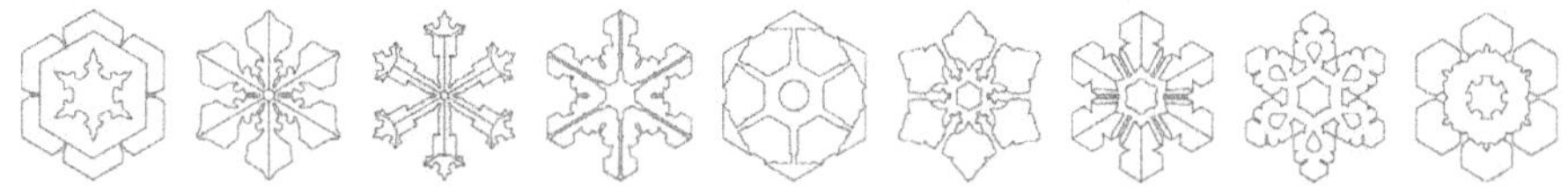

You can use colored pencils, fine point markers or crayons to color in
these designs. It's a good idea to put a blank sheet of paper behind the
page you are coloring so the colors don't go through to the next page.

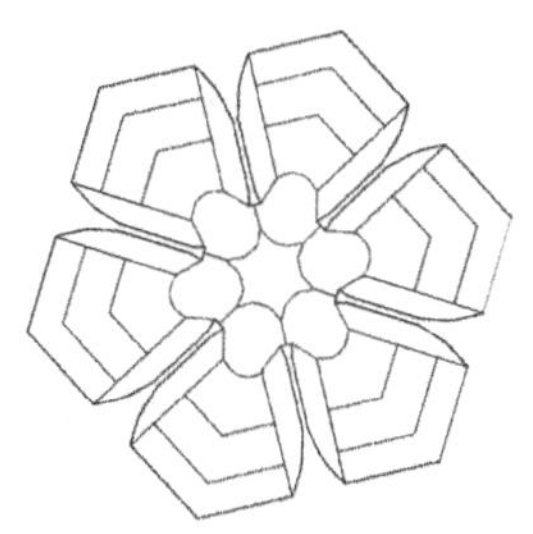
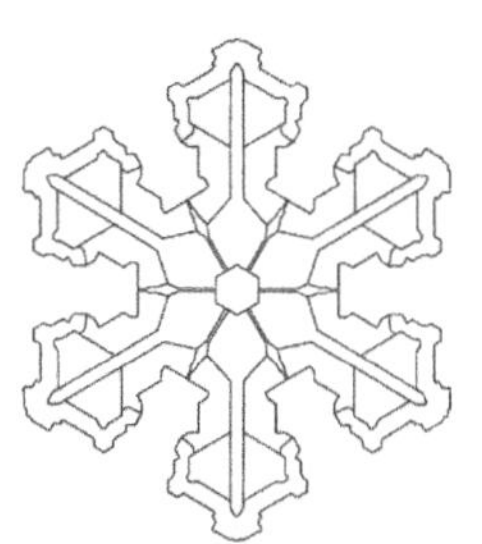
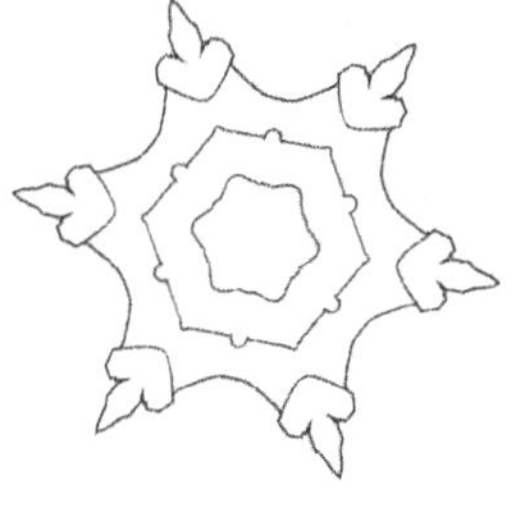

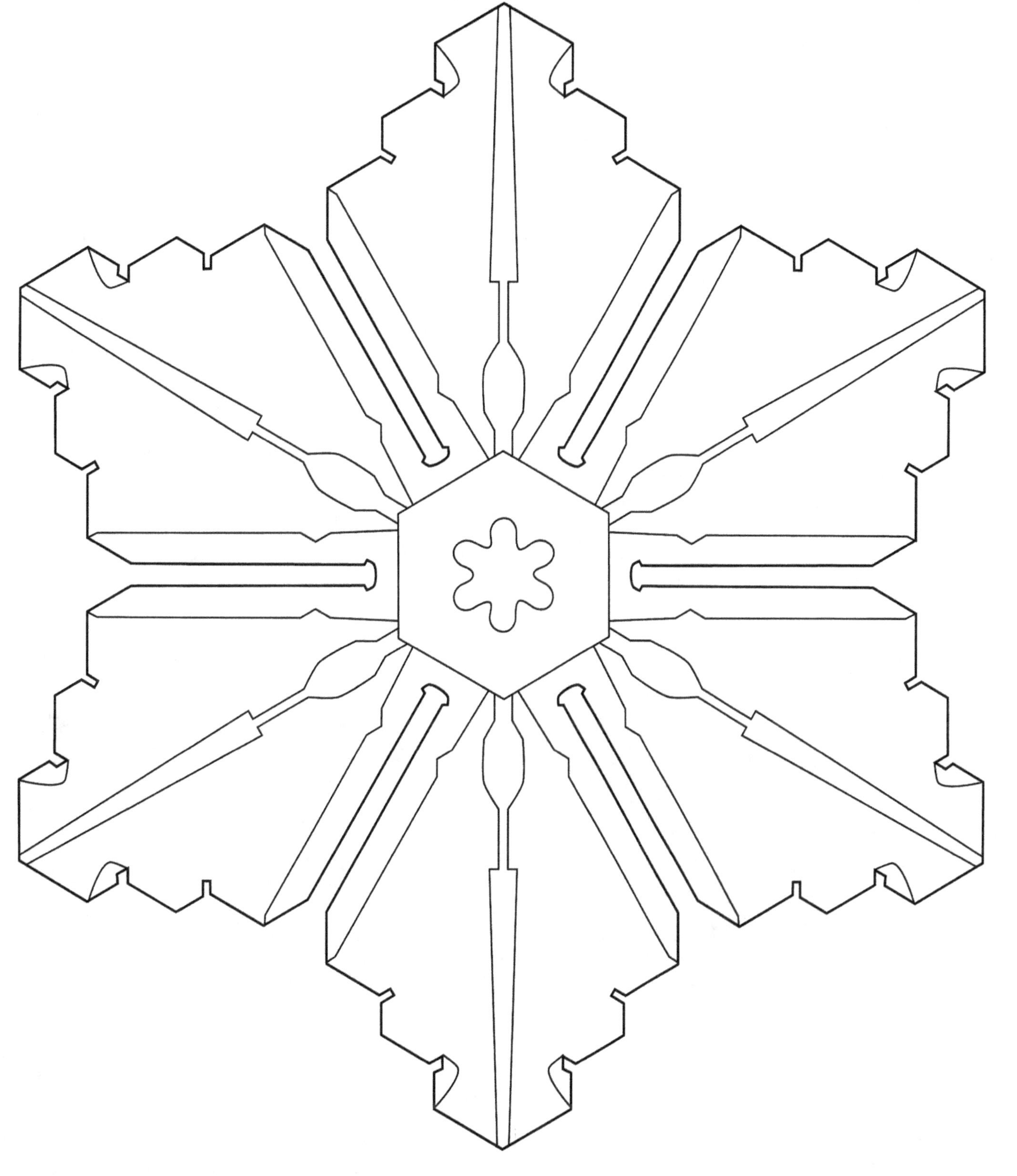

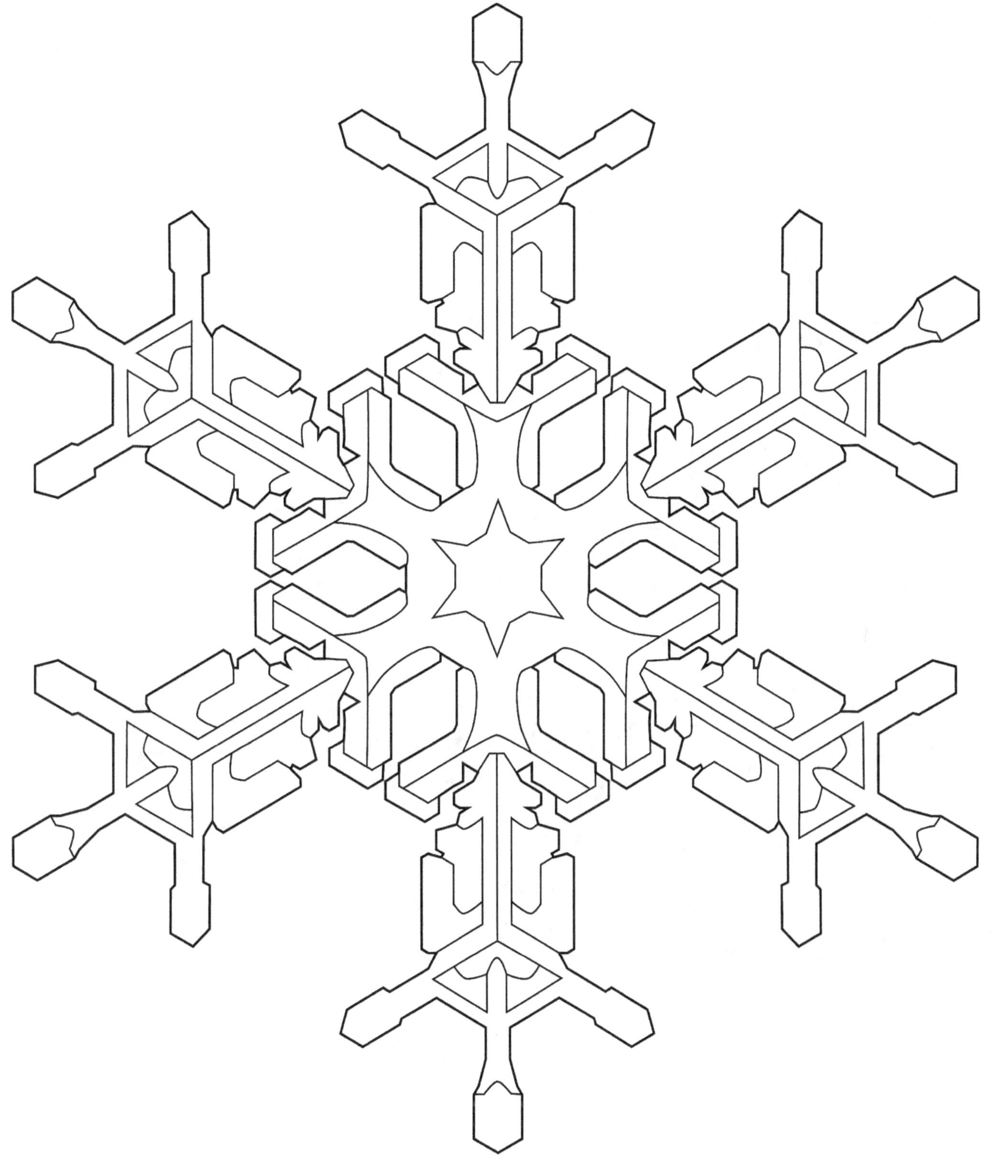

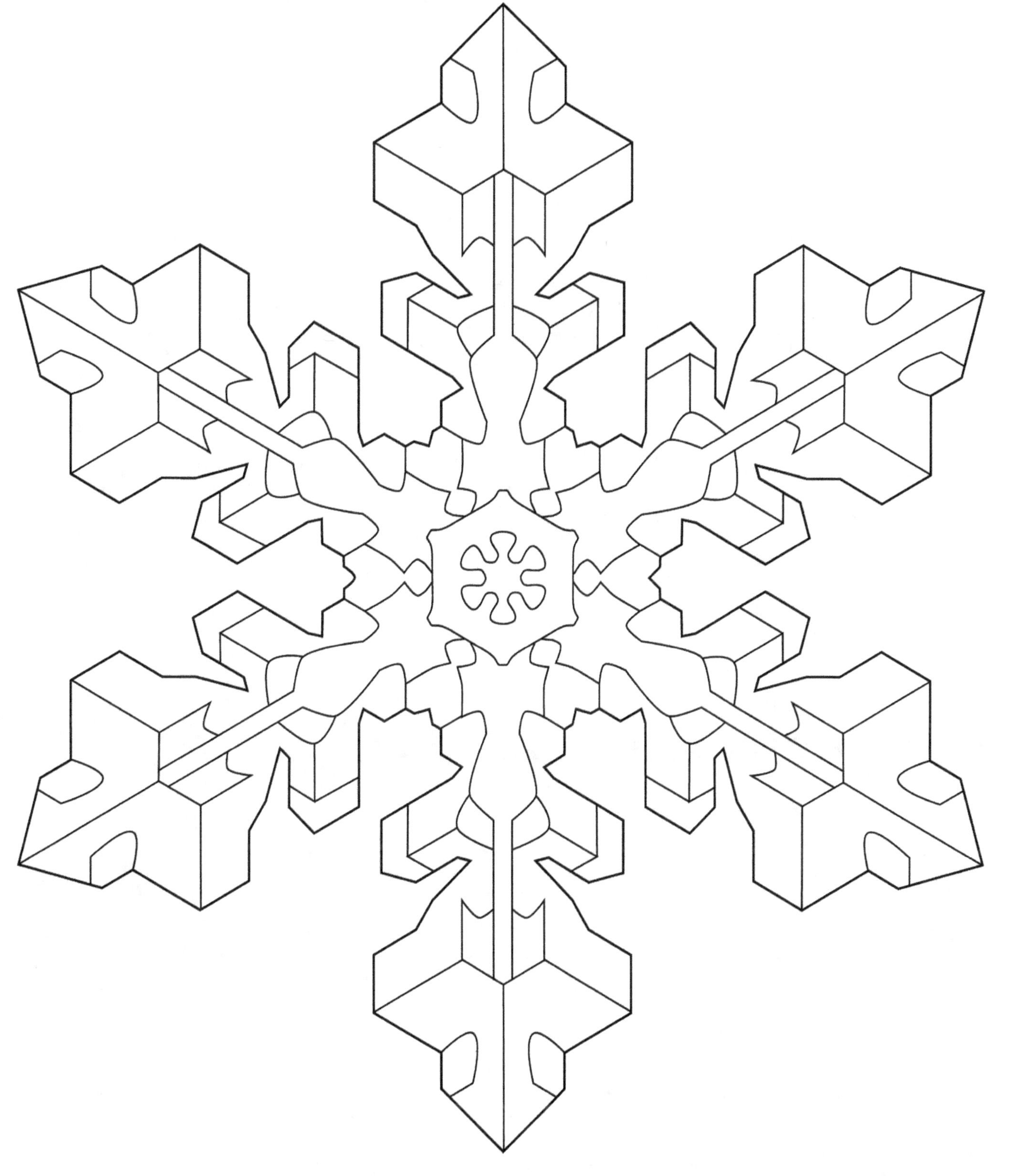

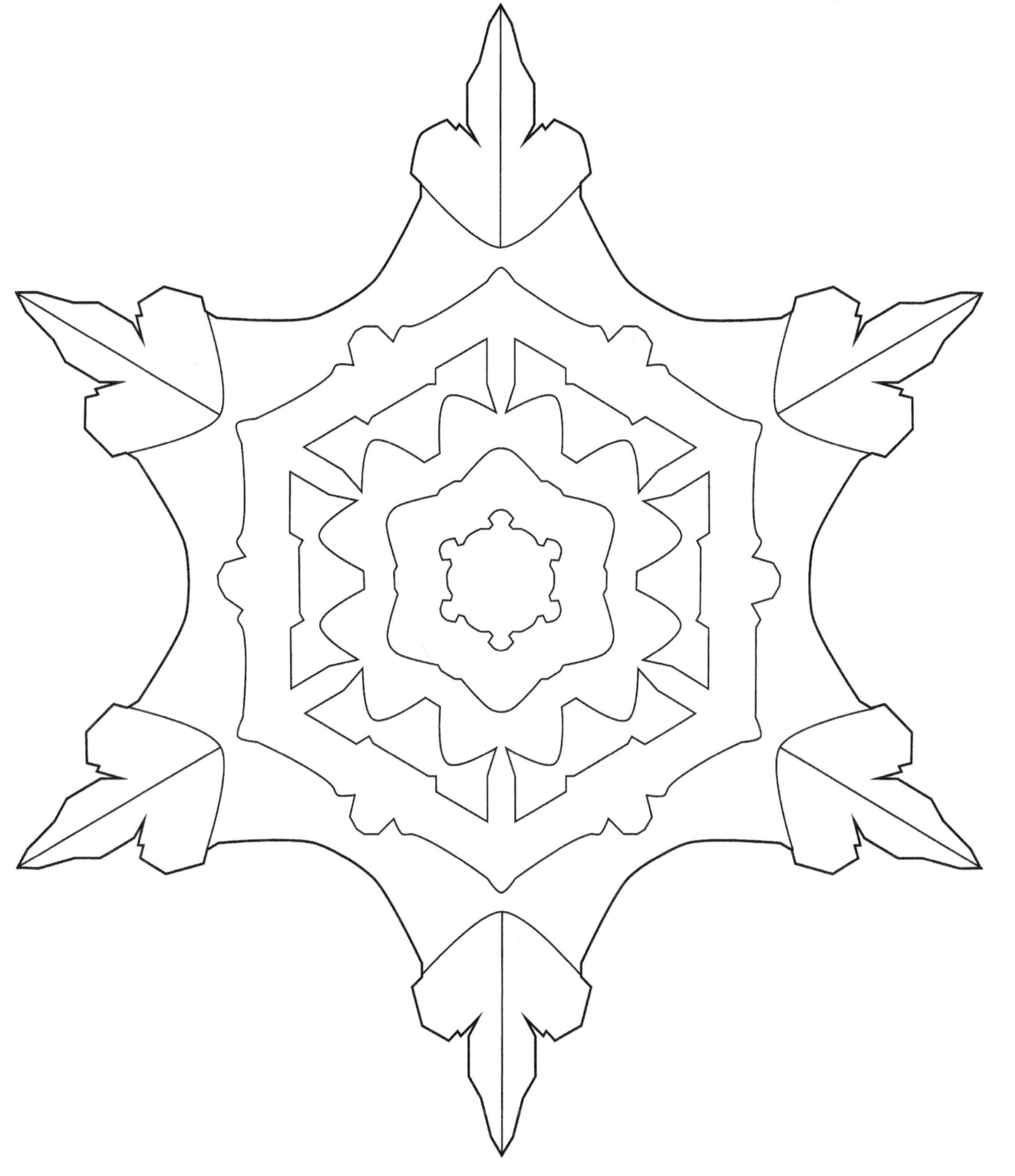

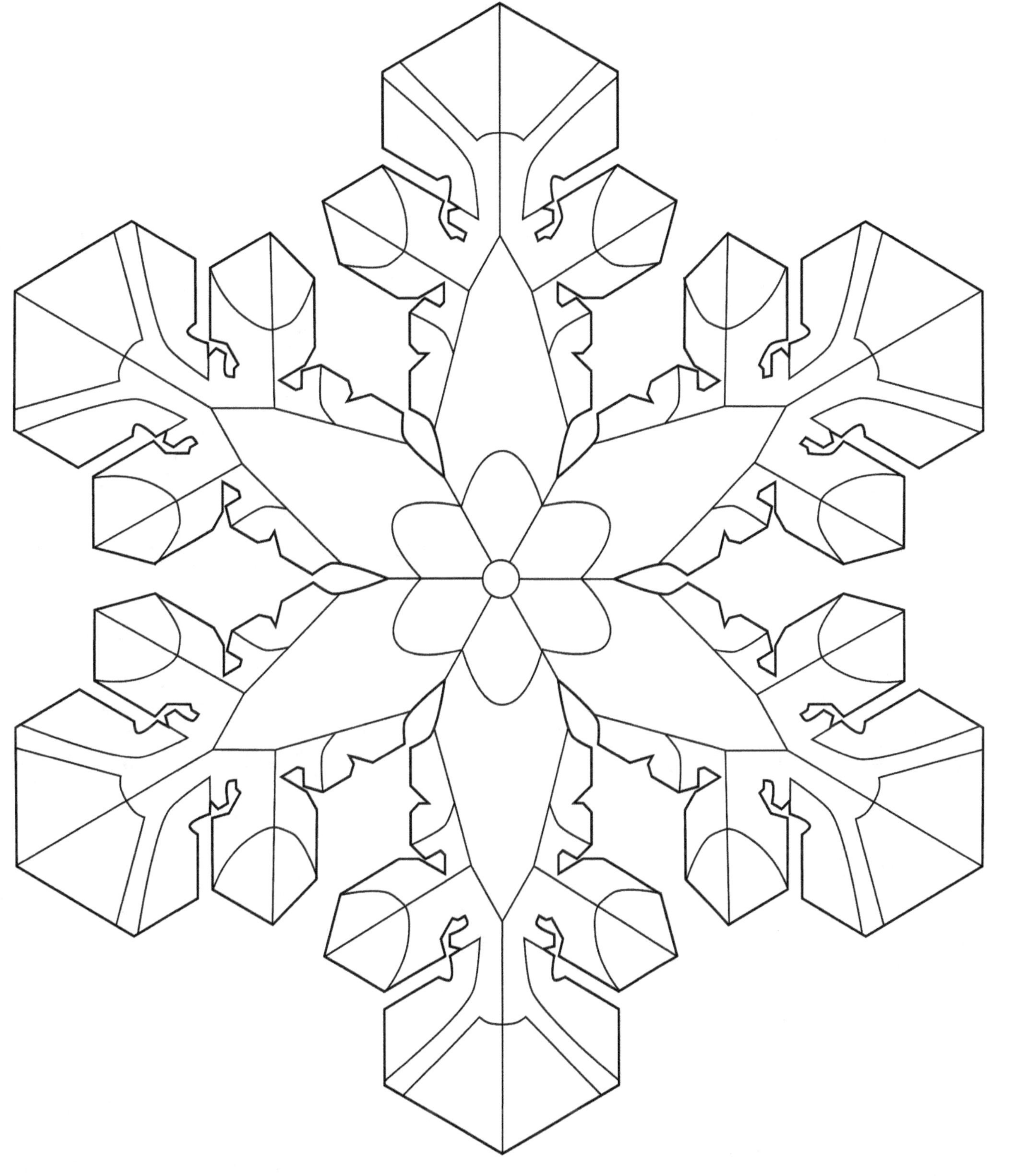

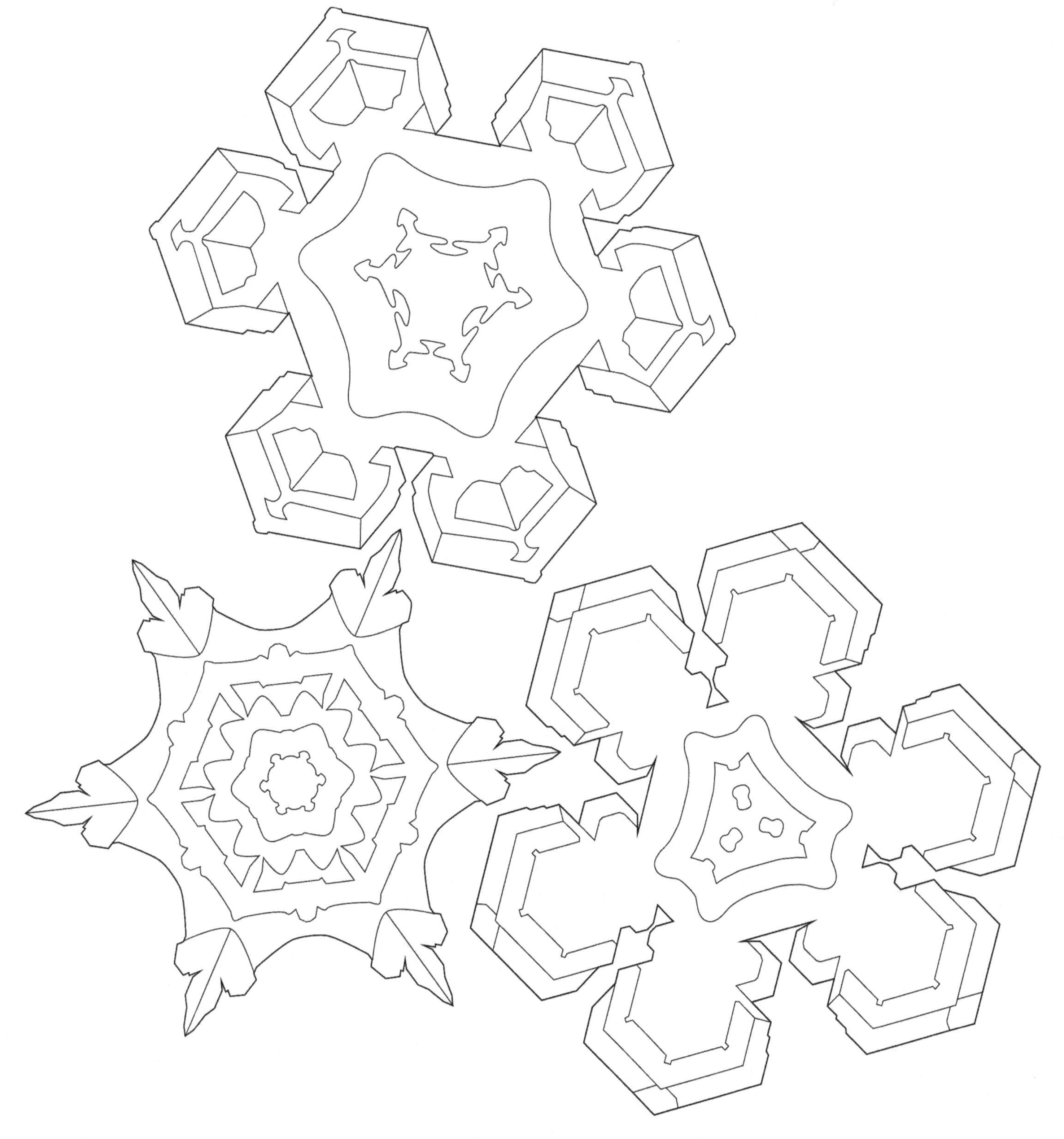

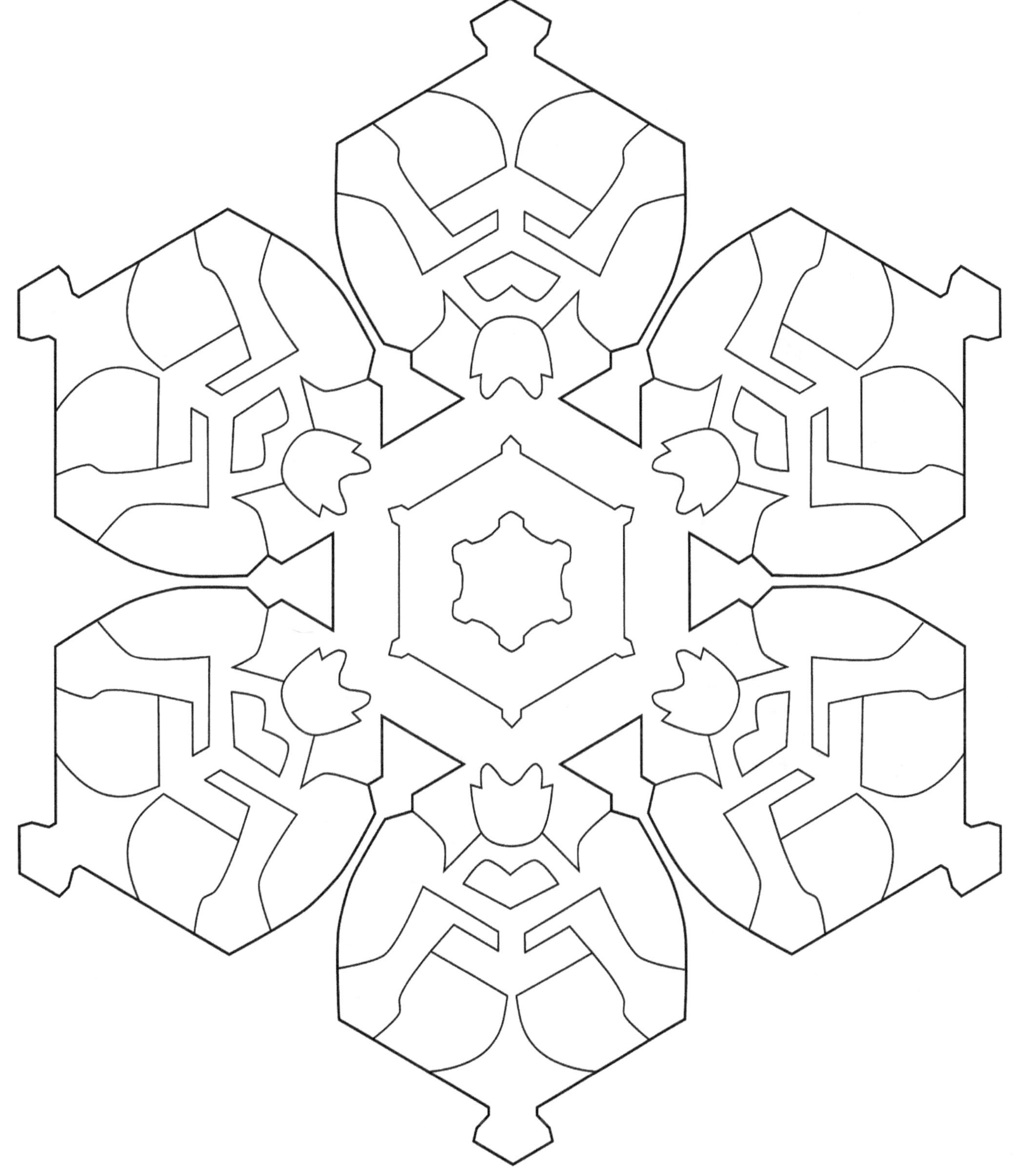

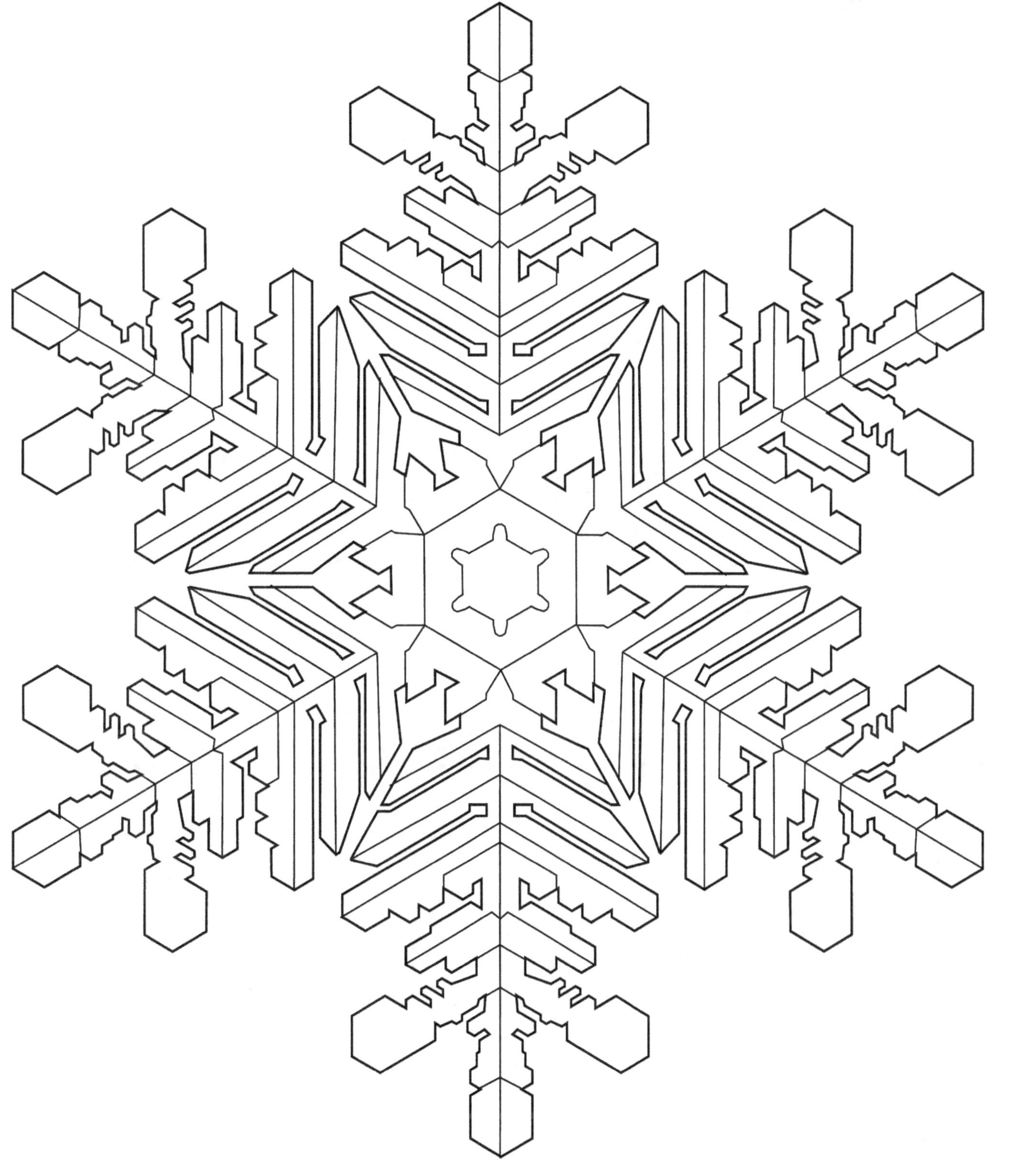

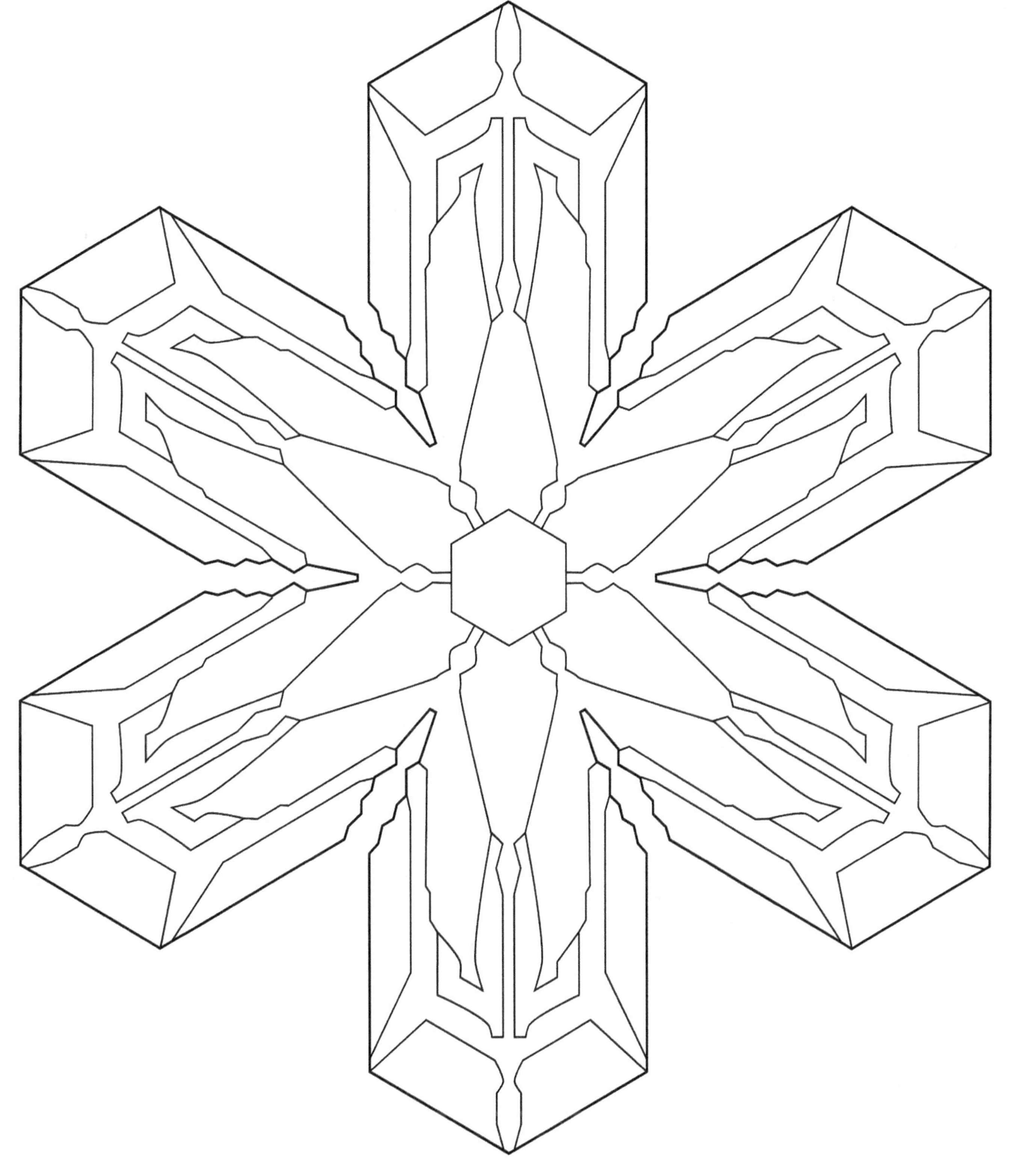

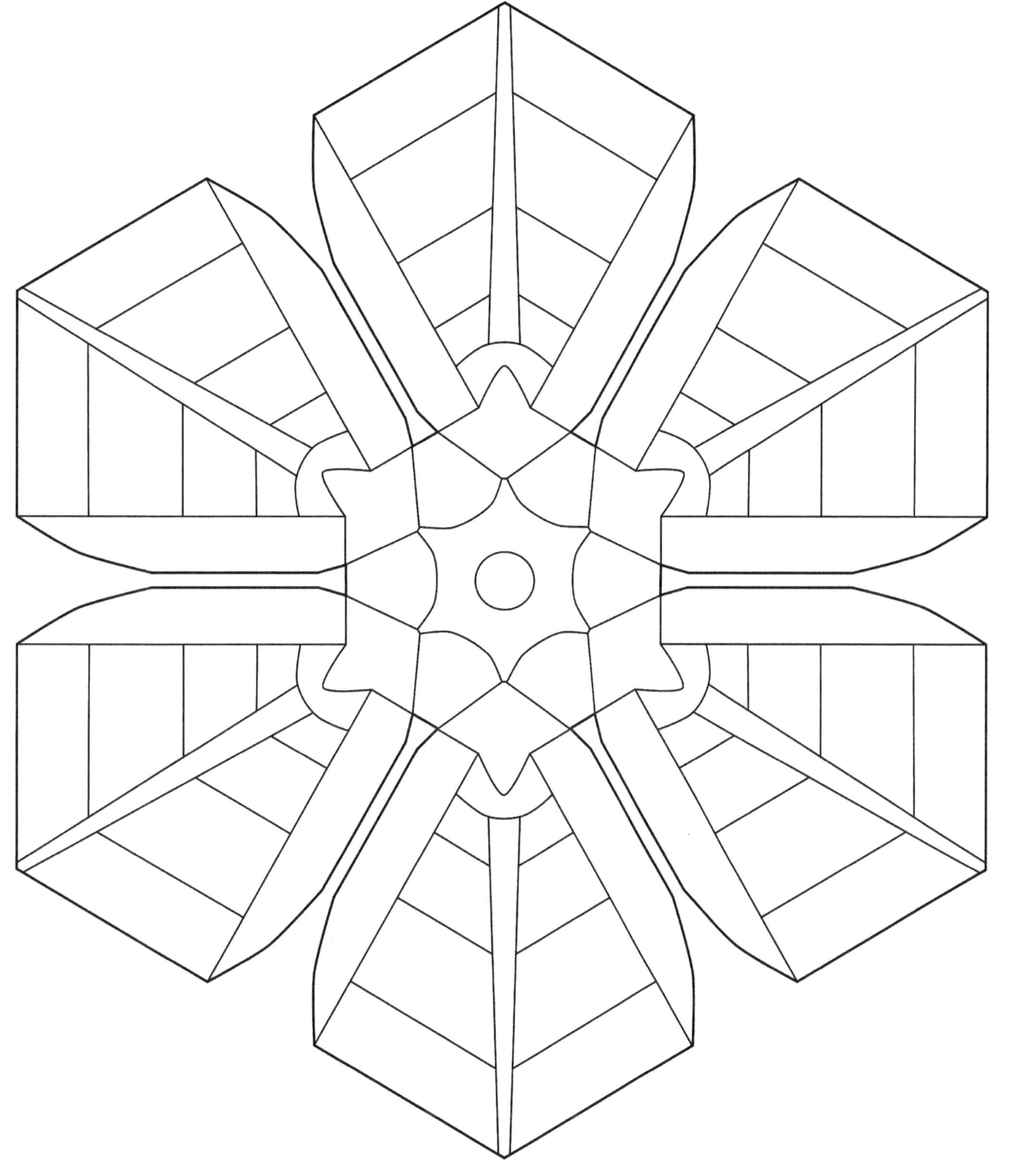

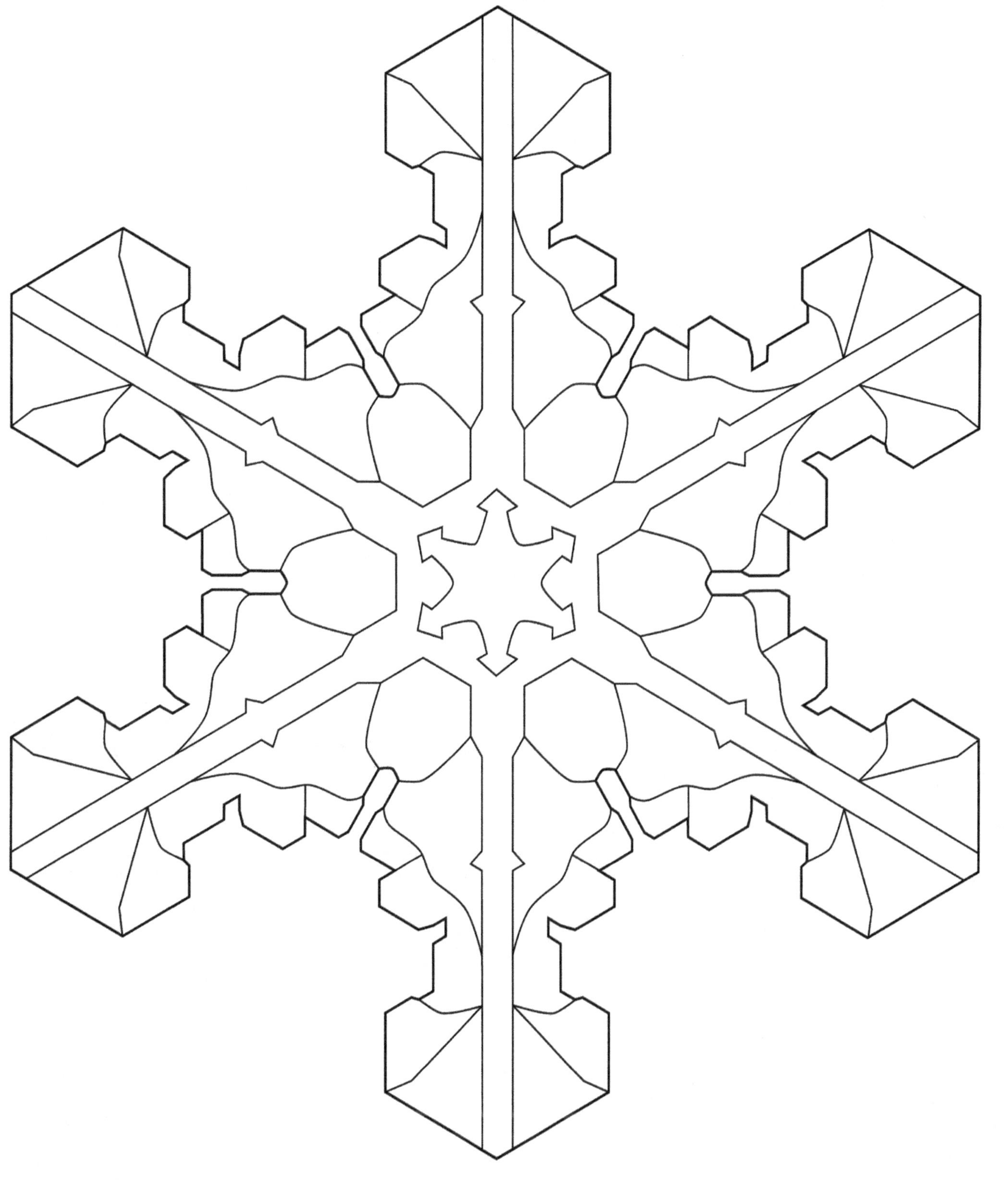

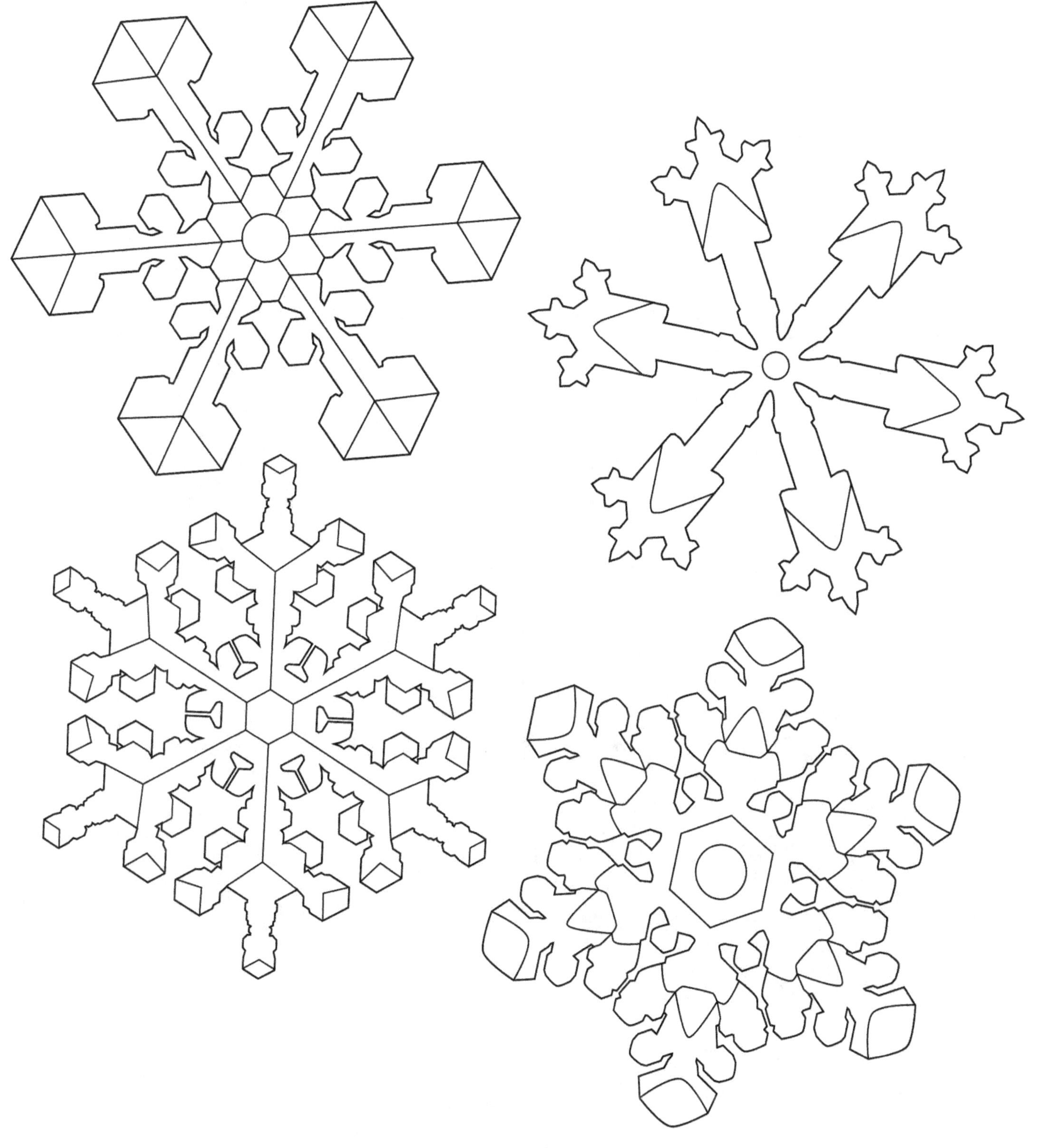

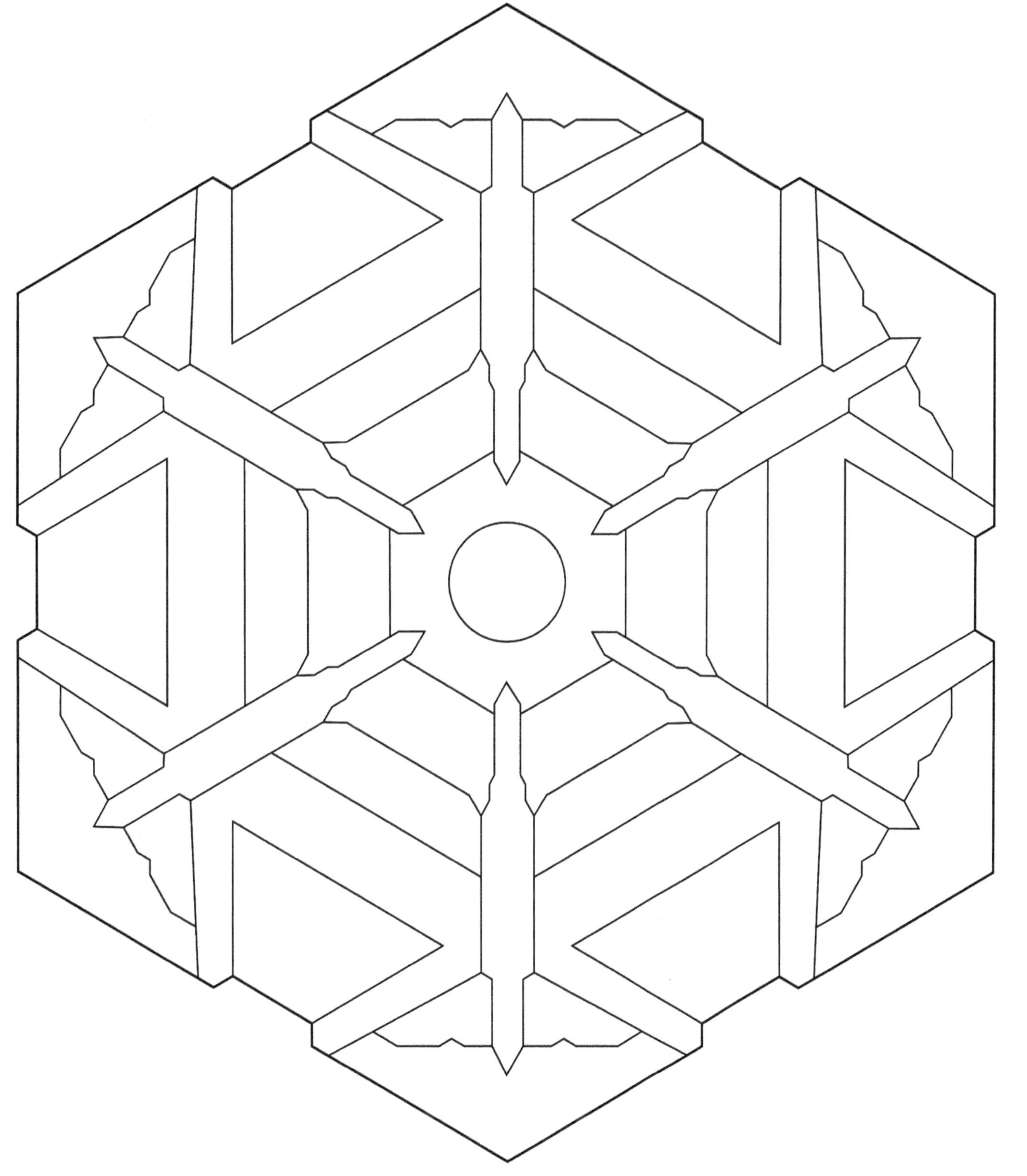

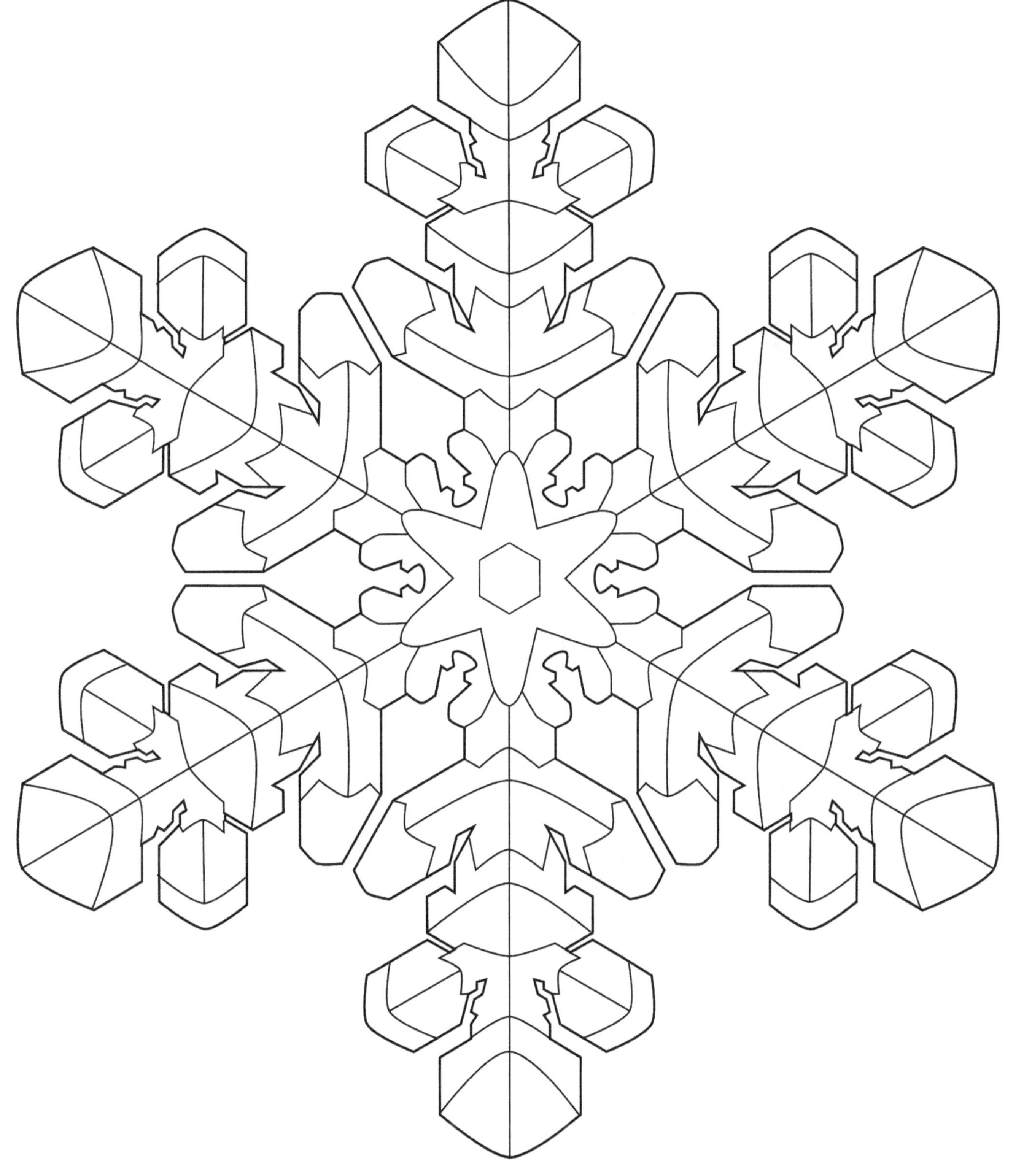

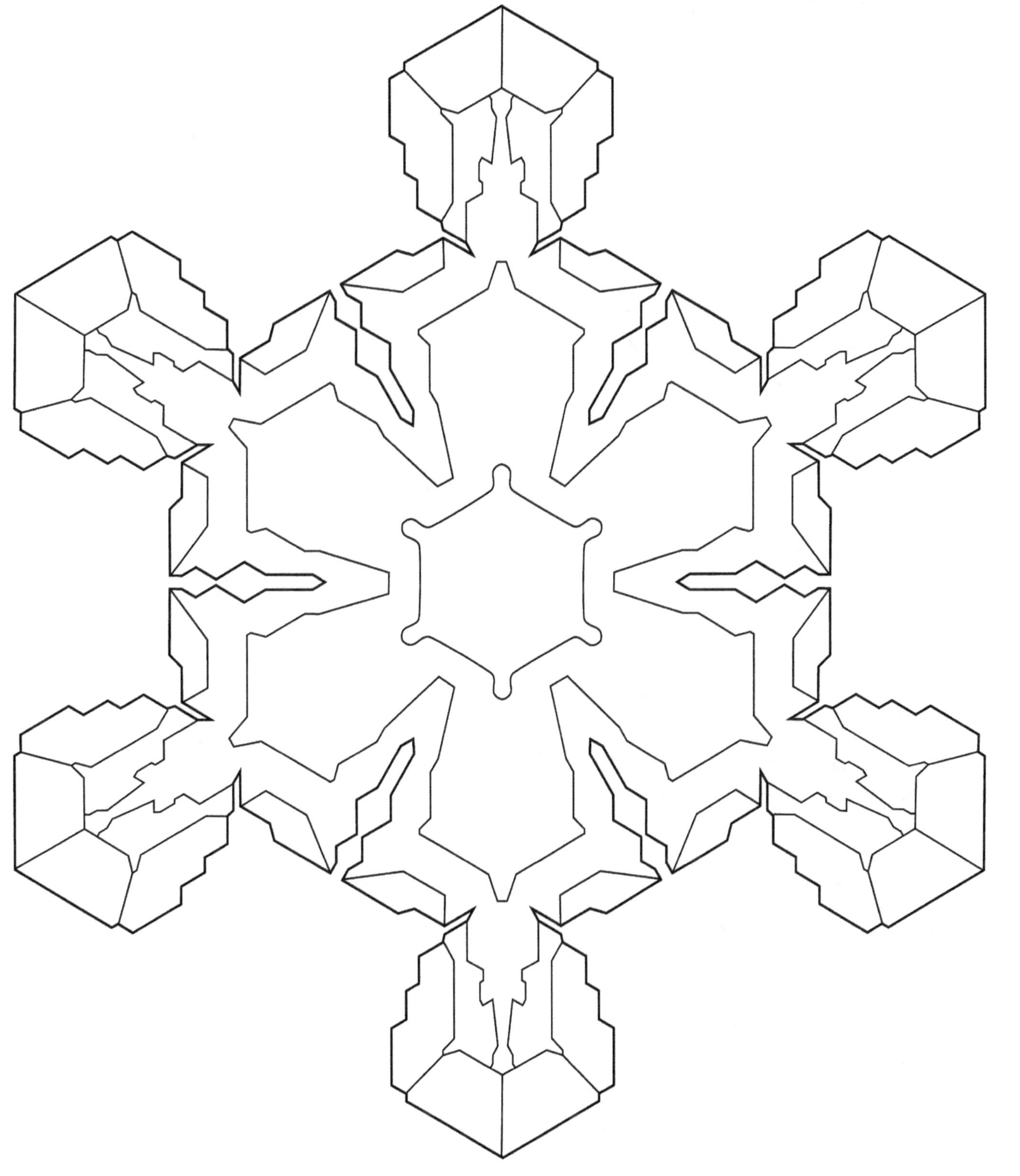

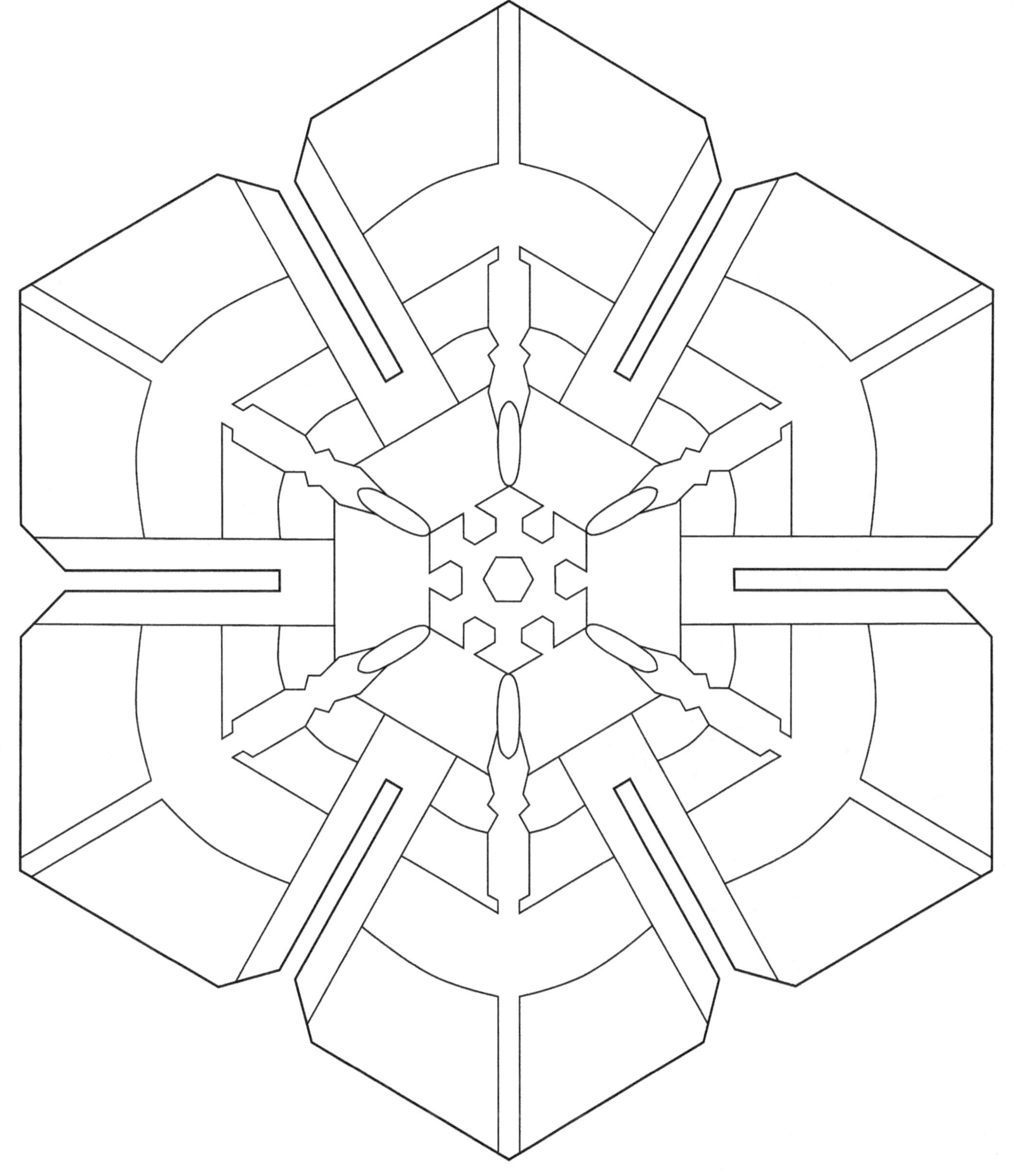

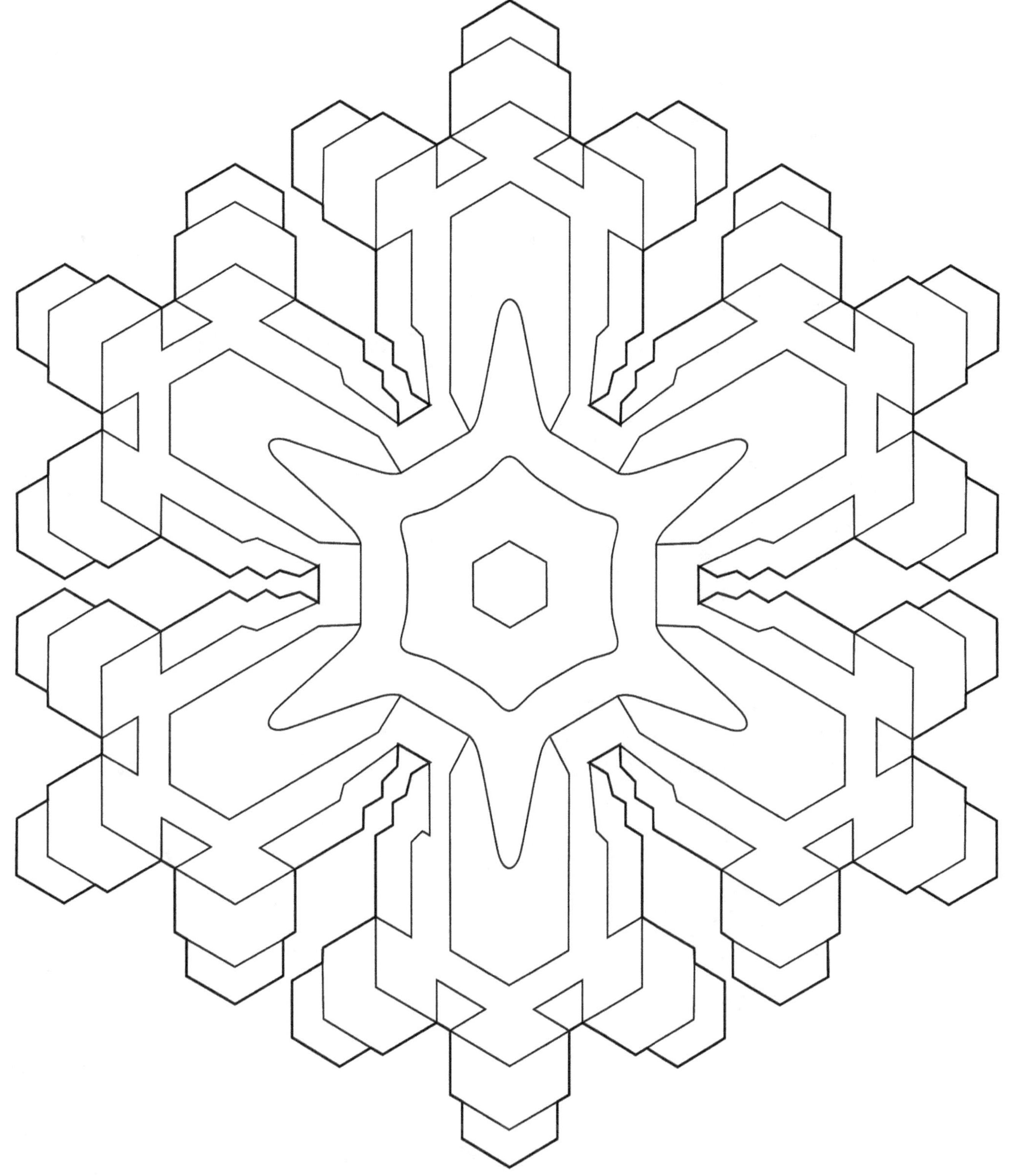

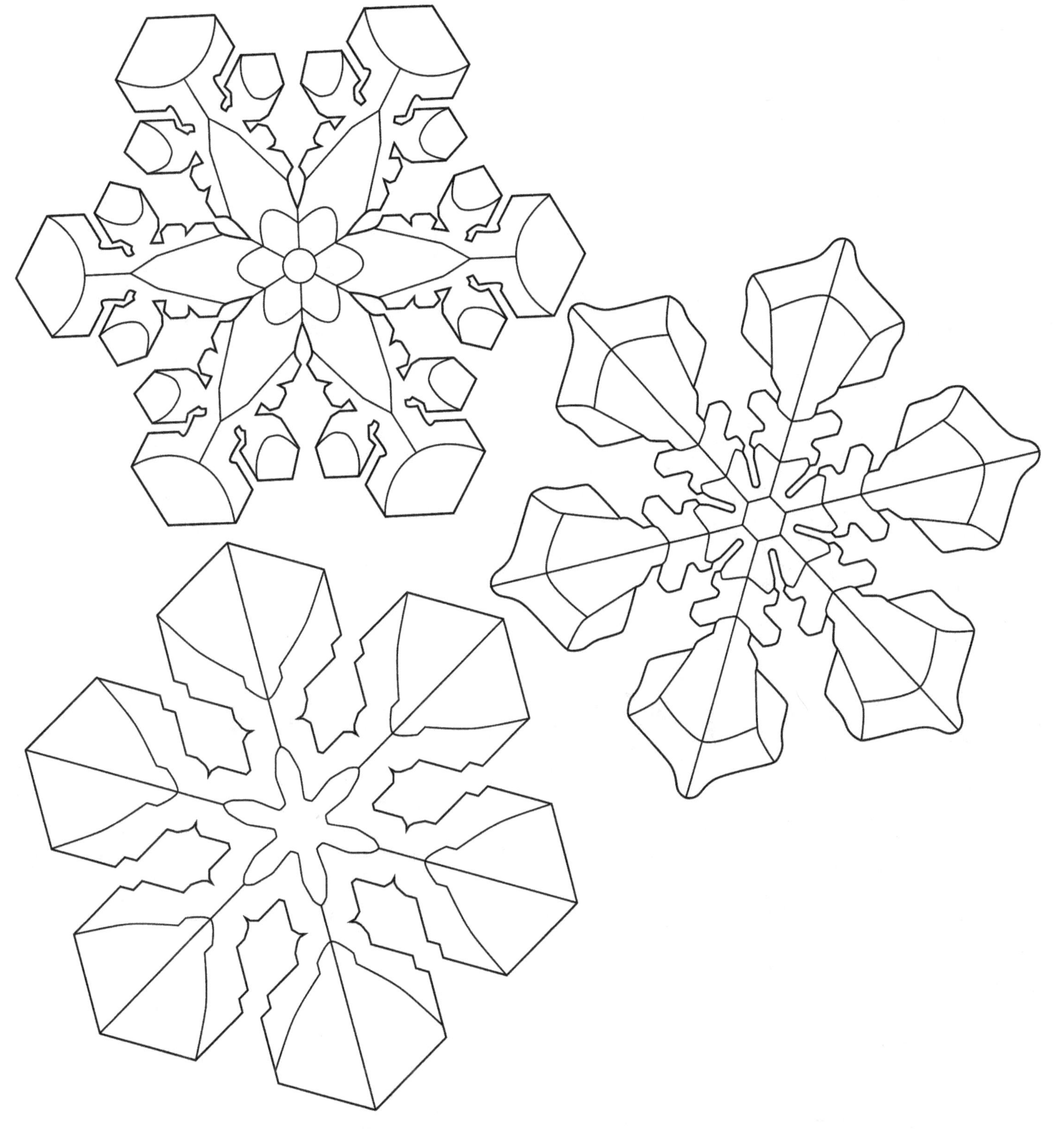

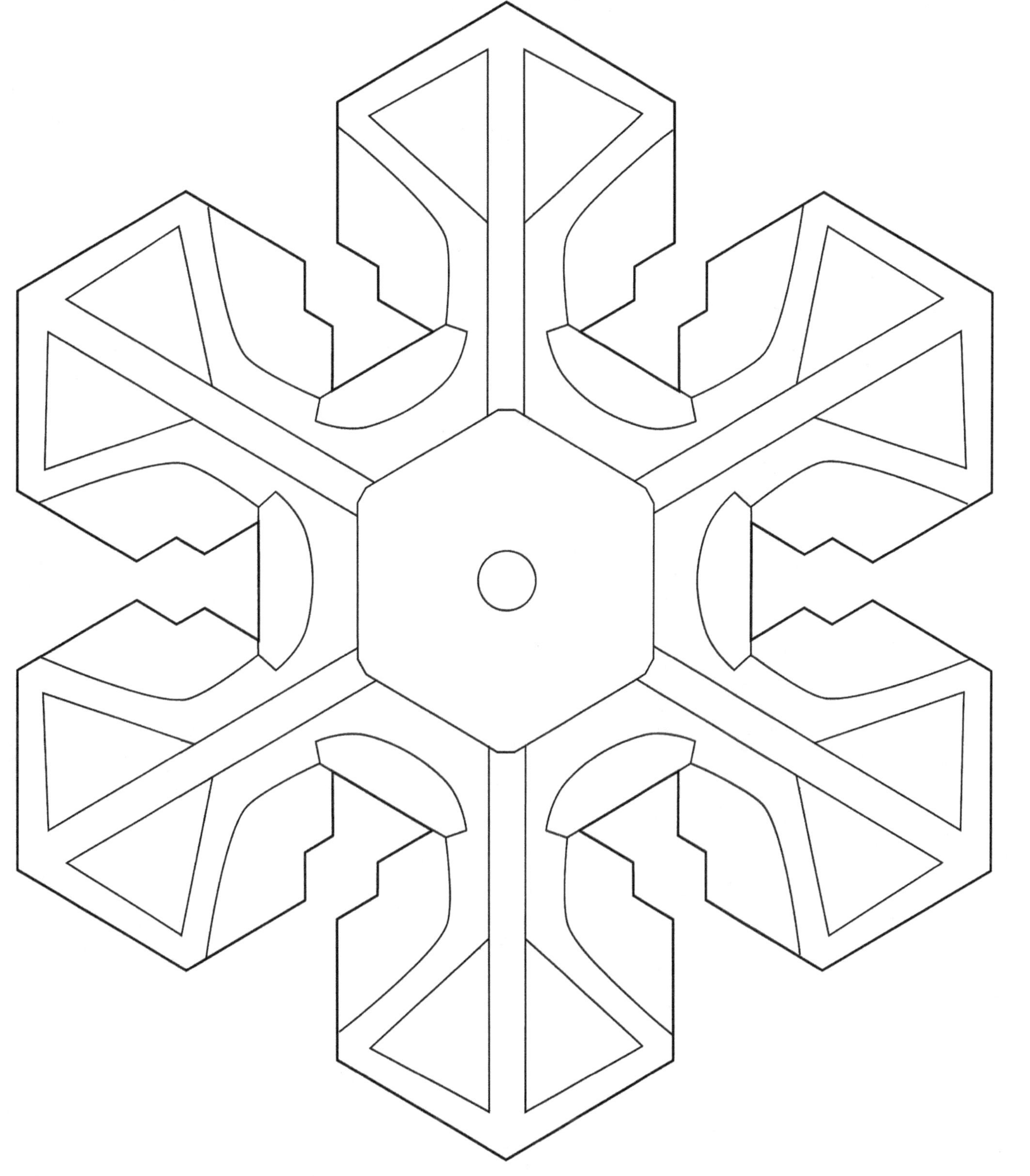

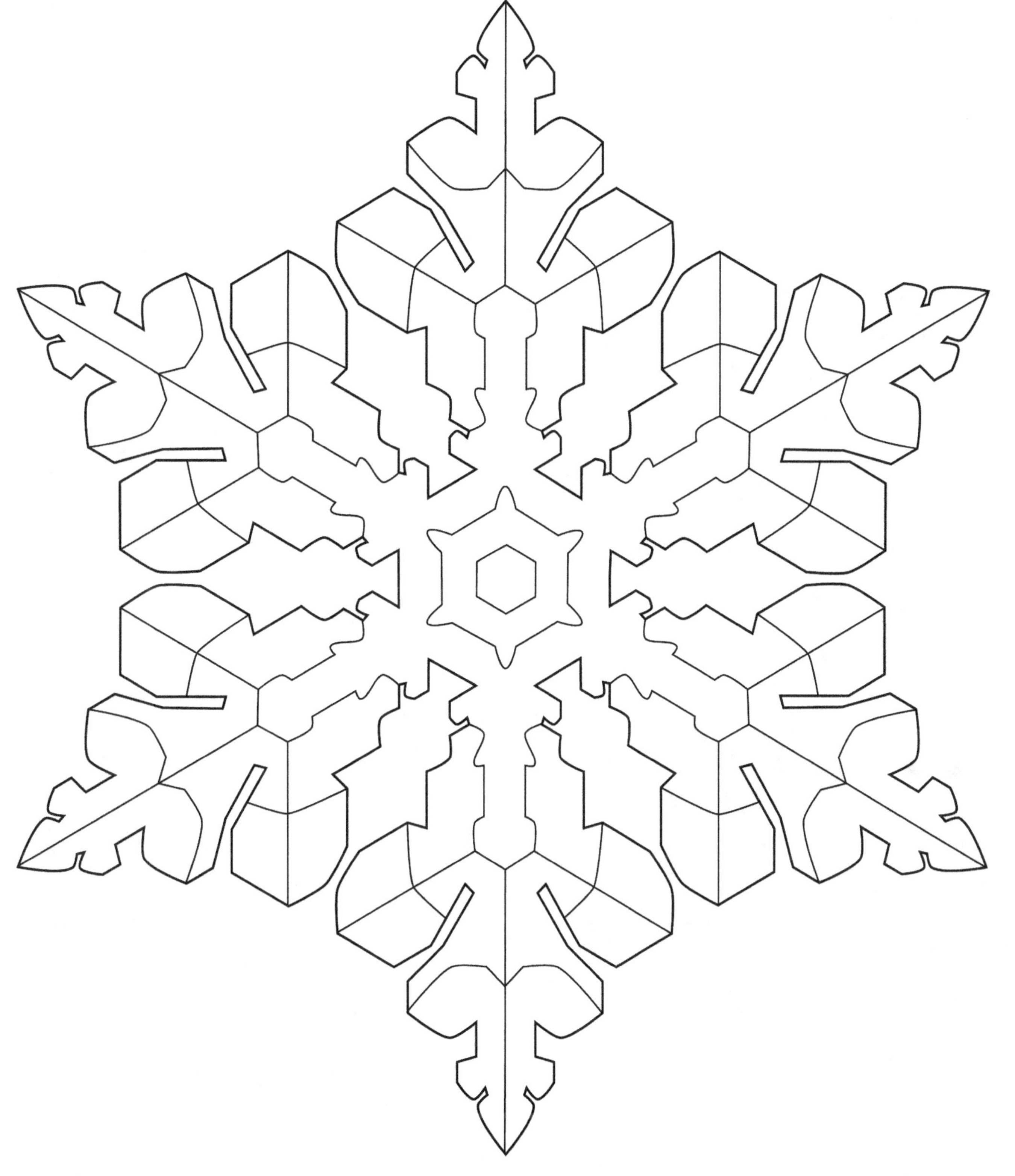

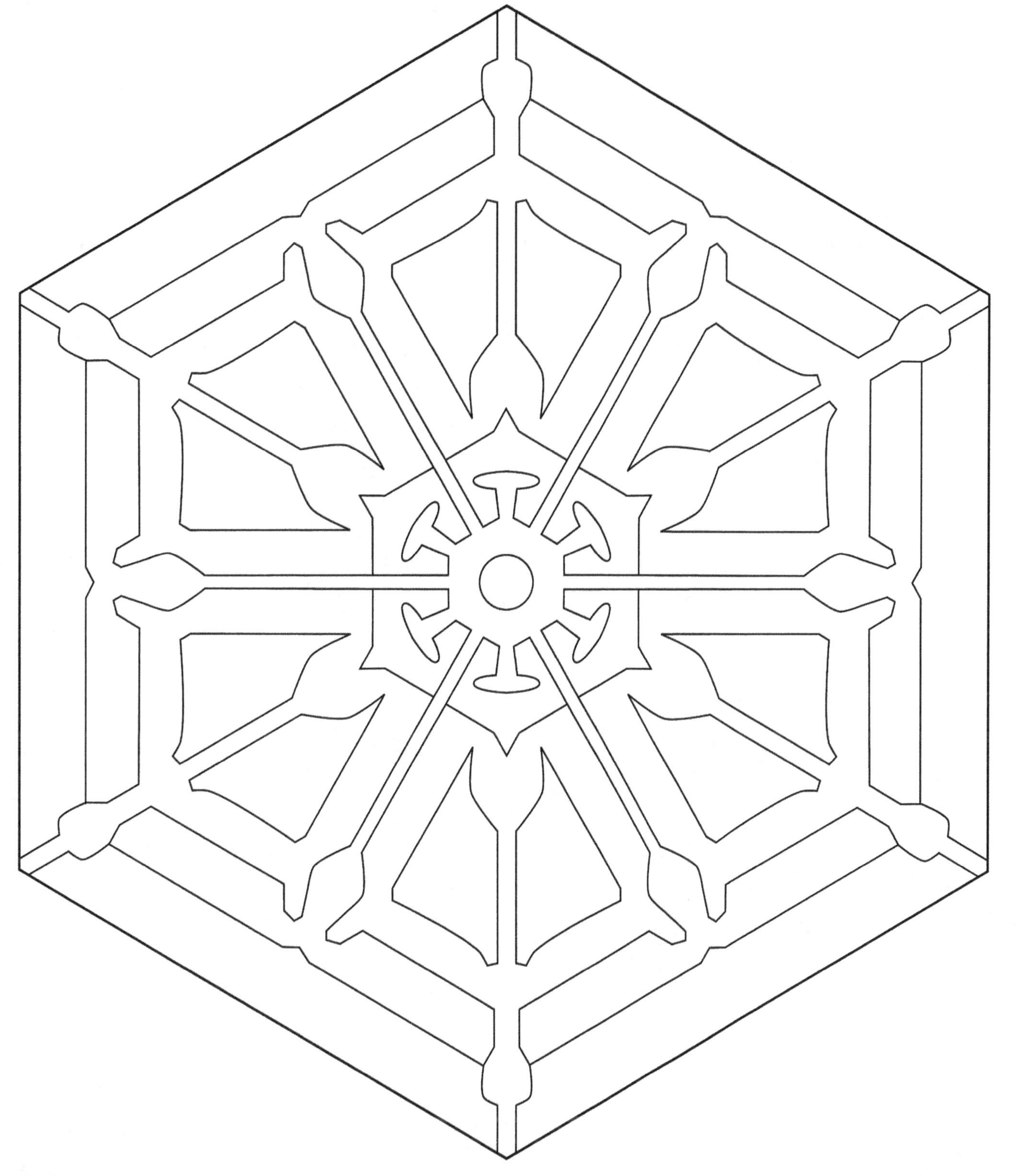

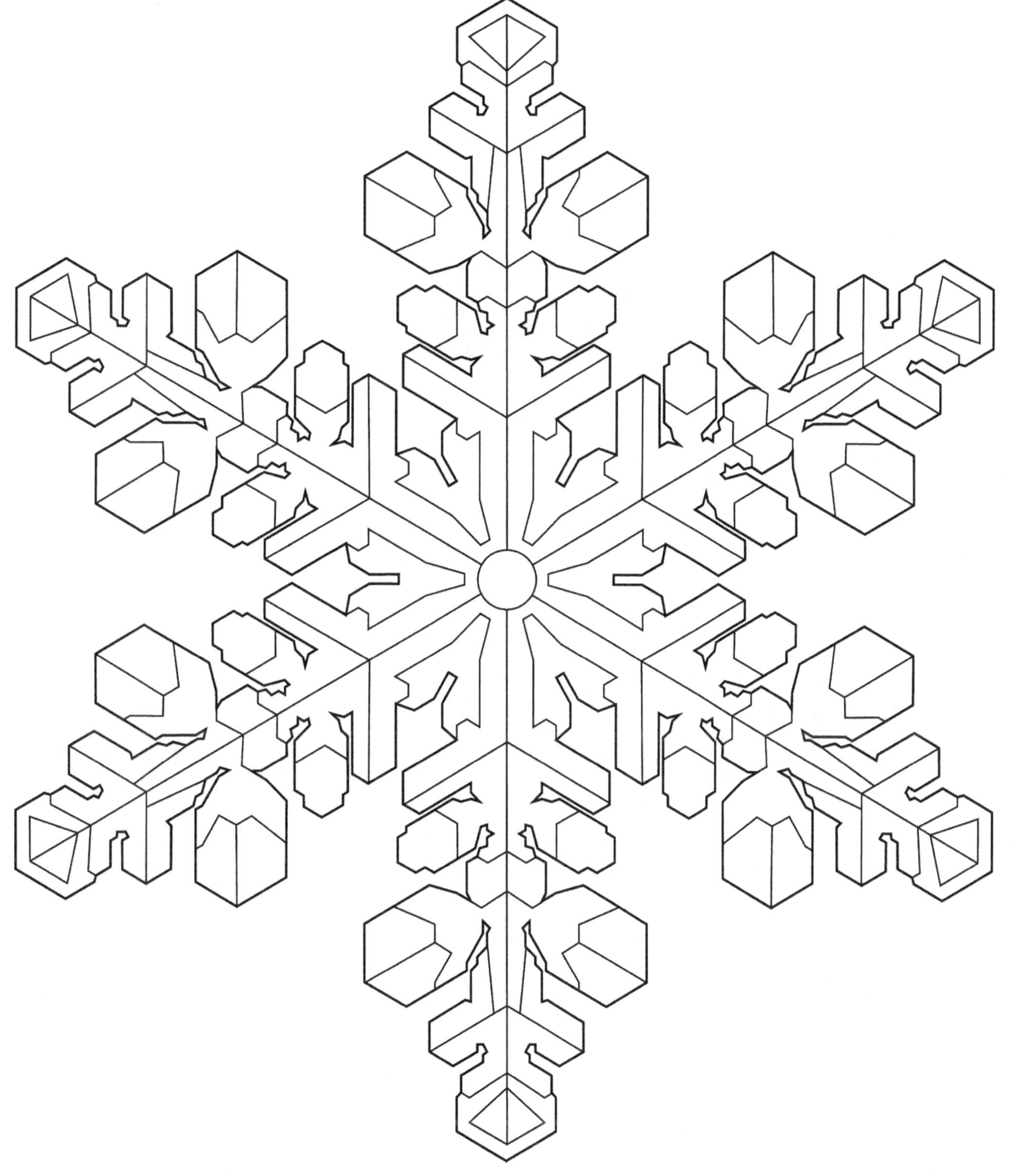

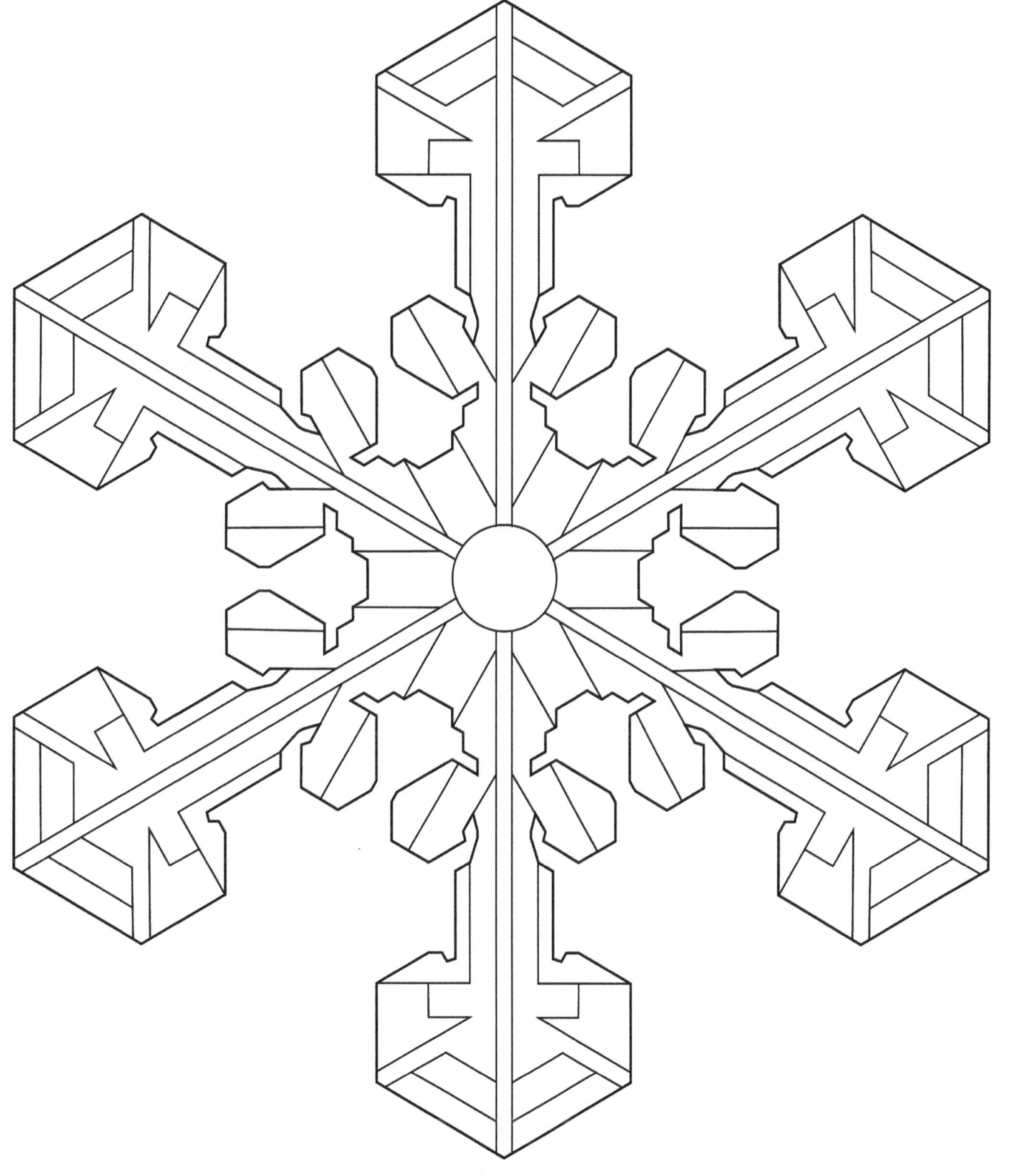

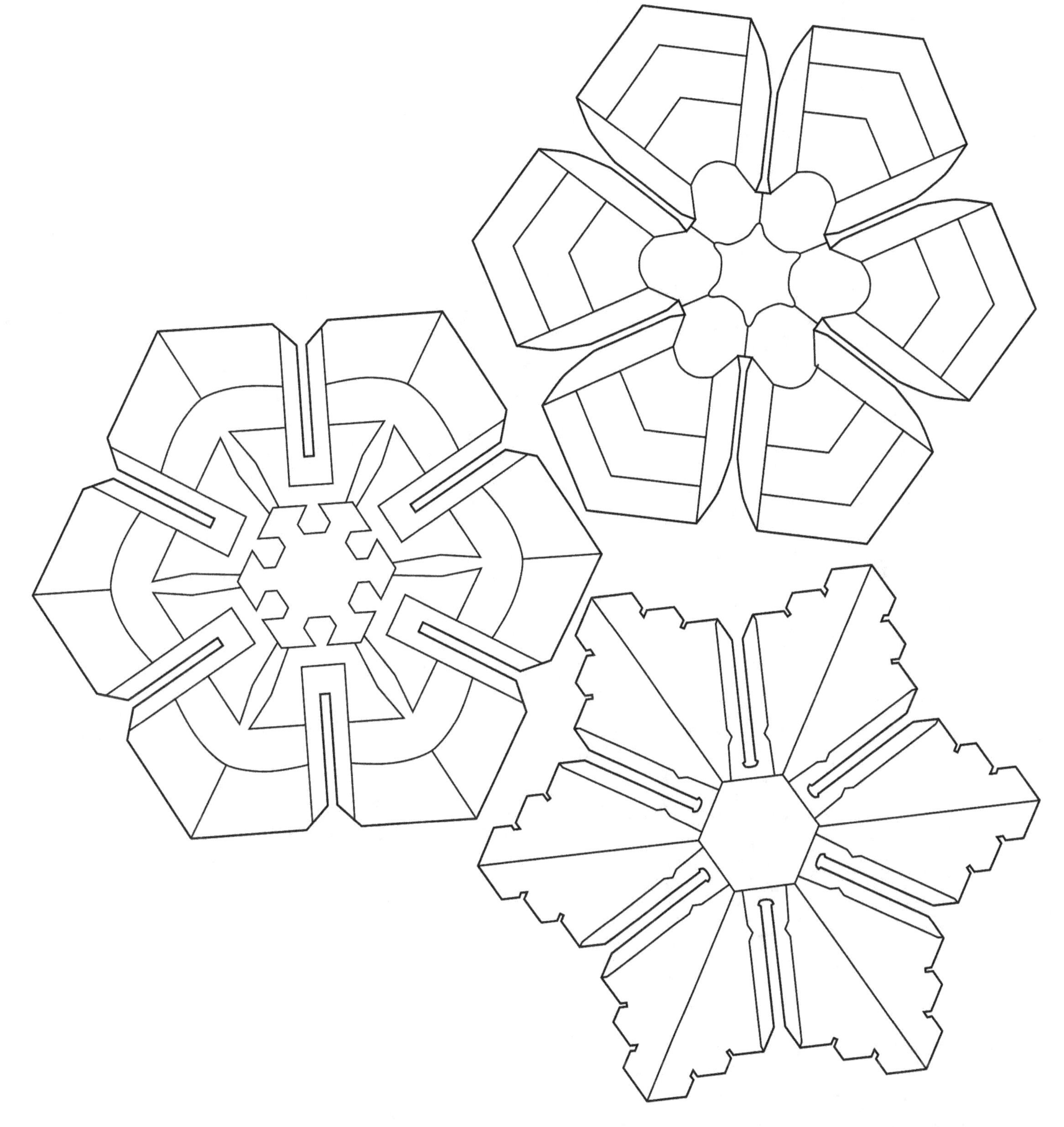

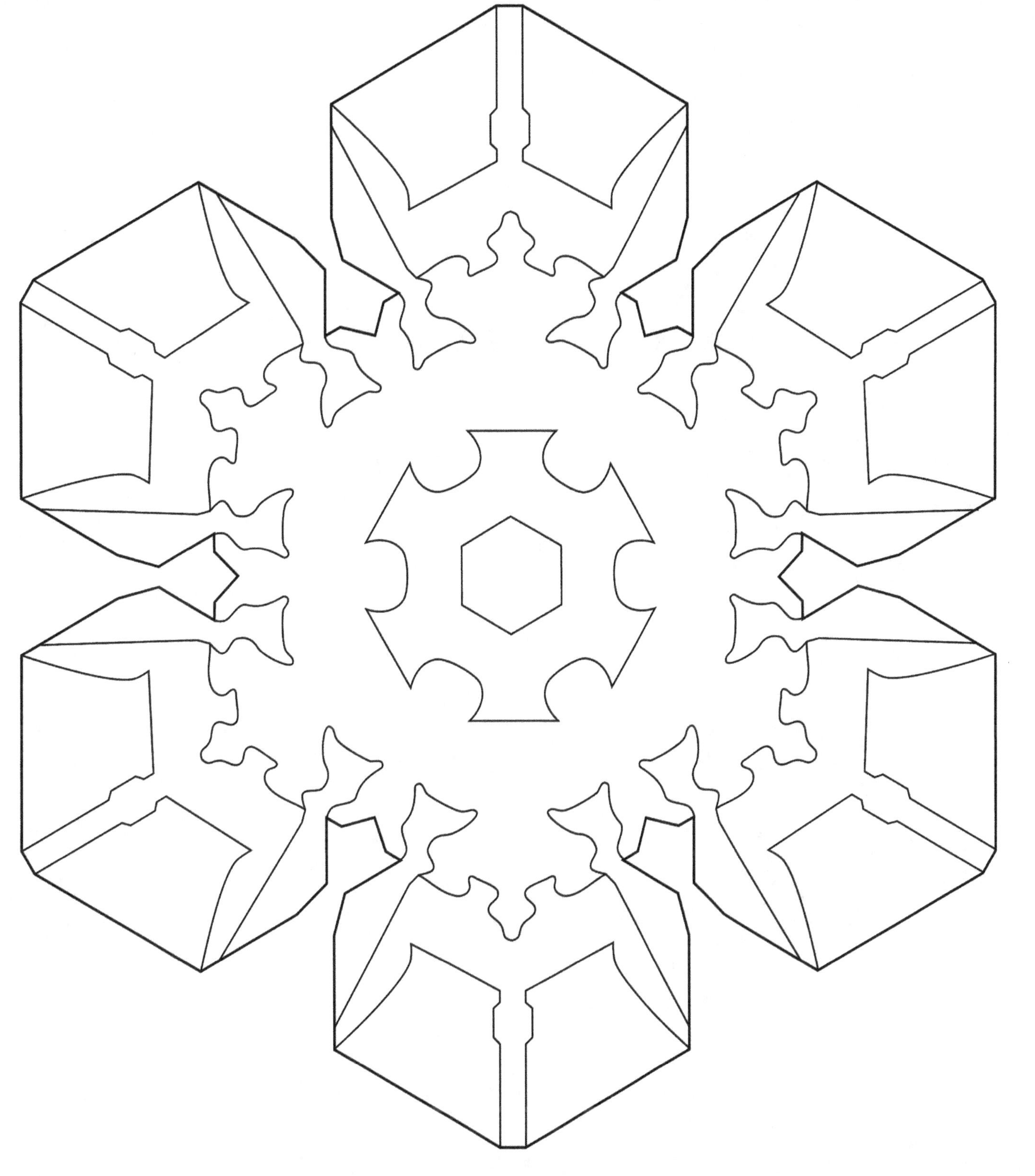

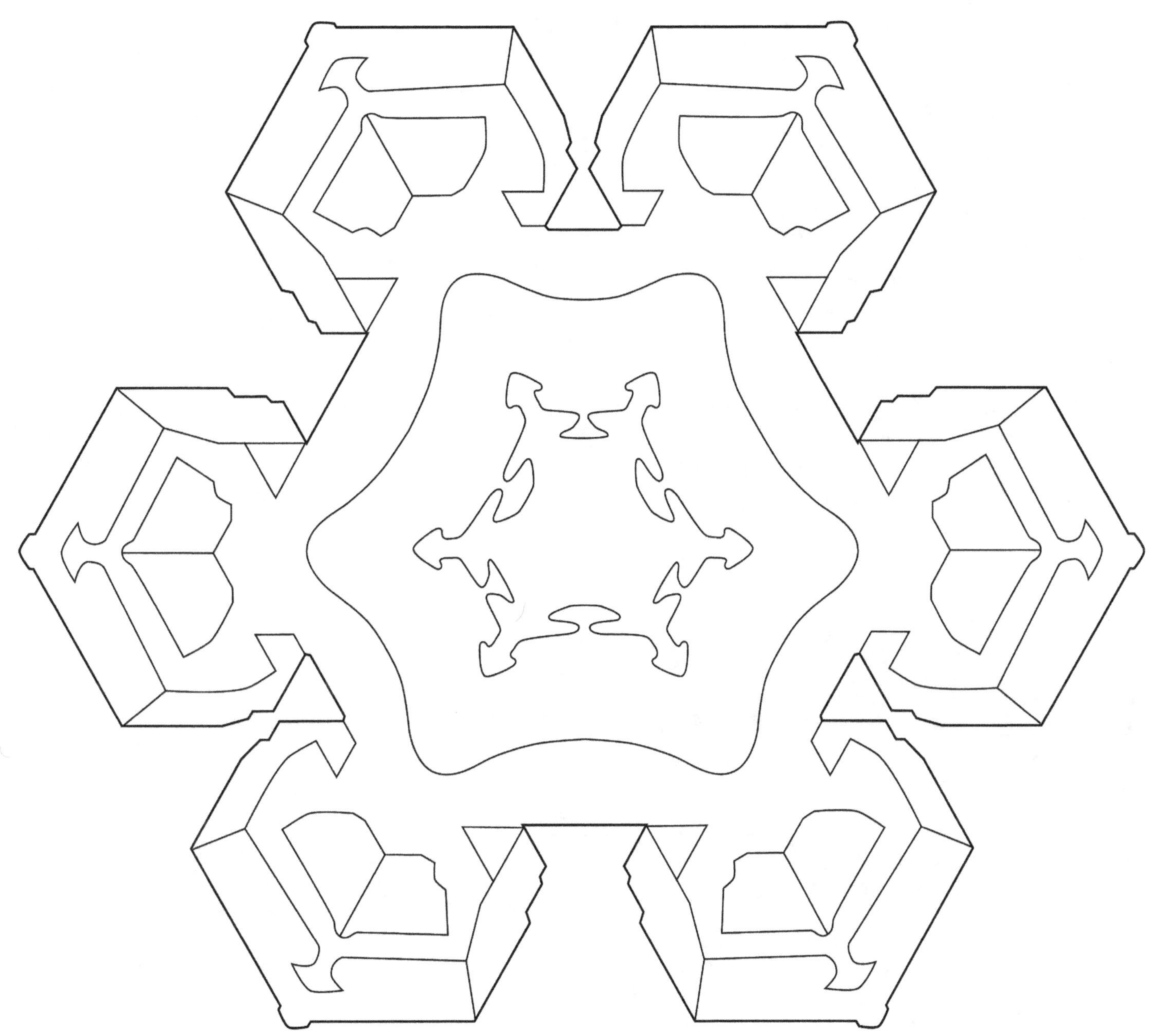

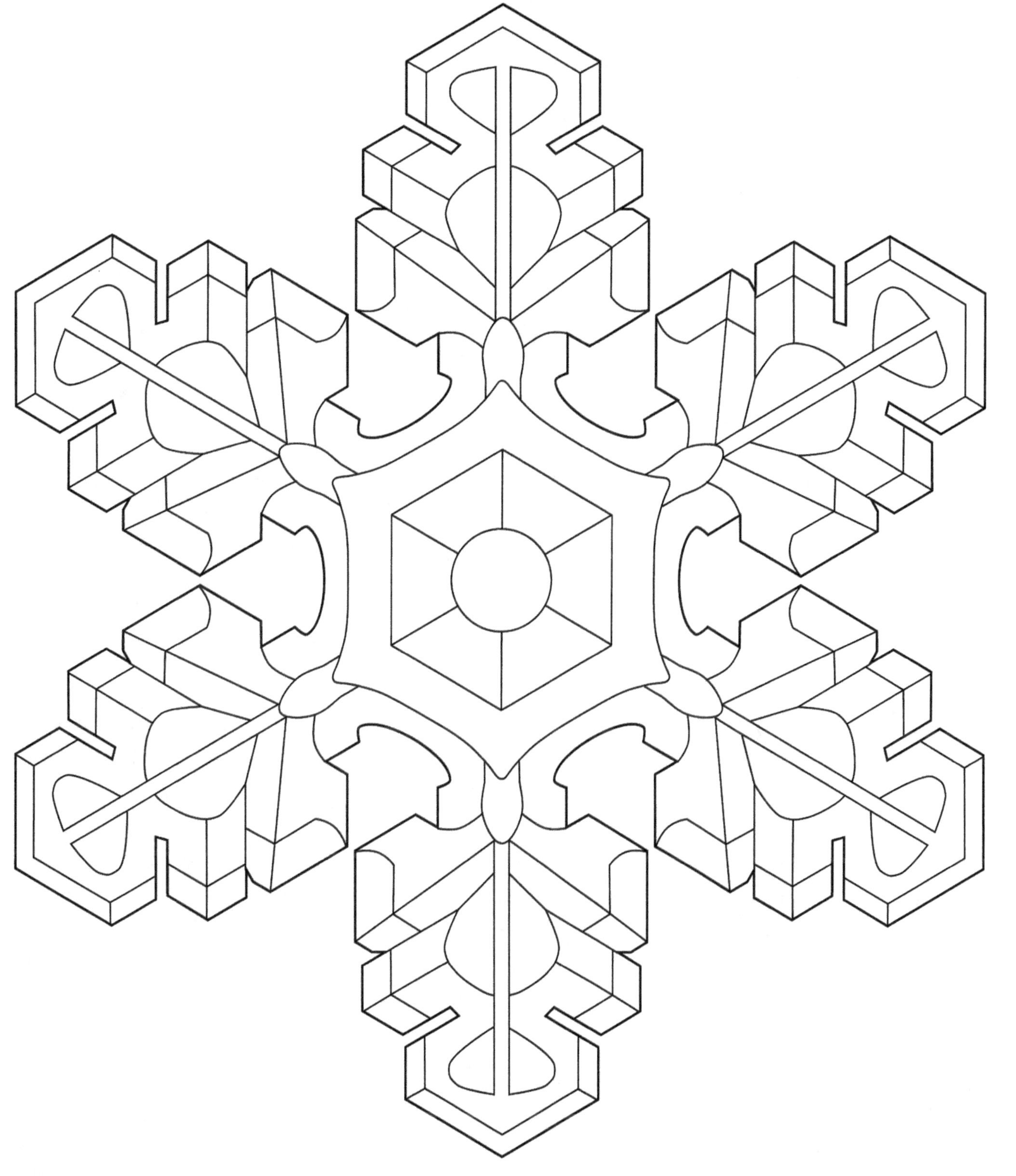

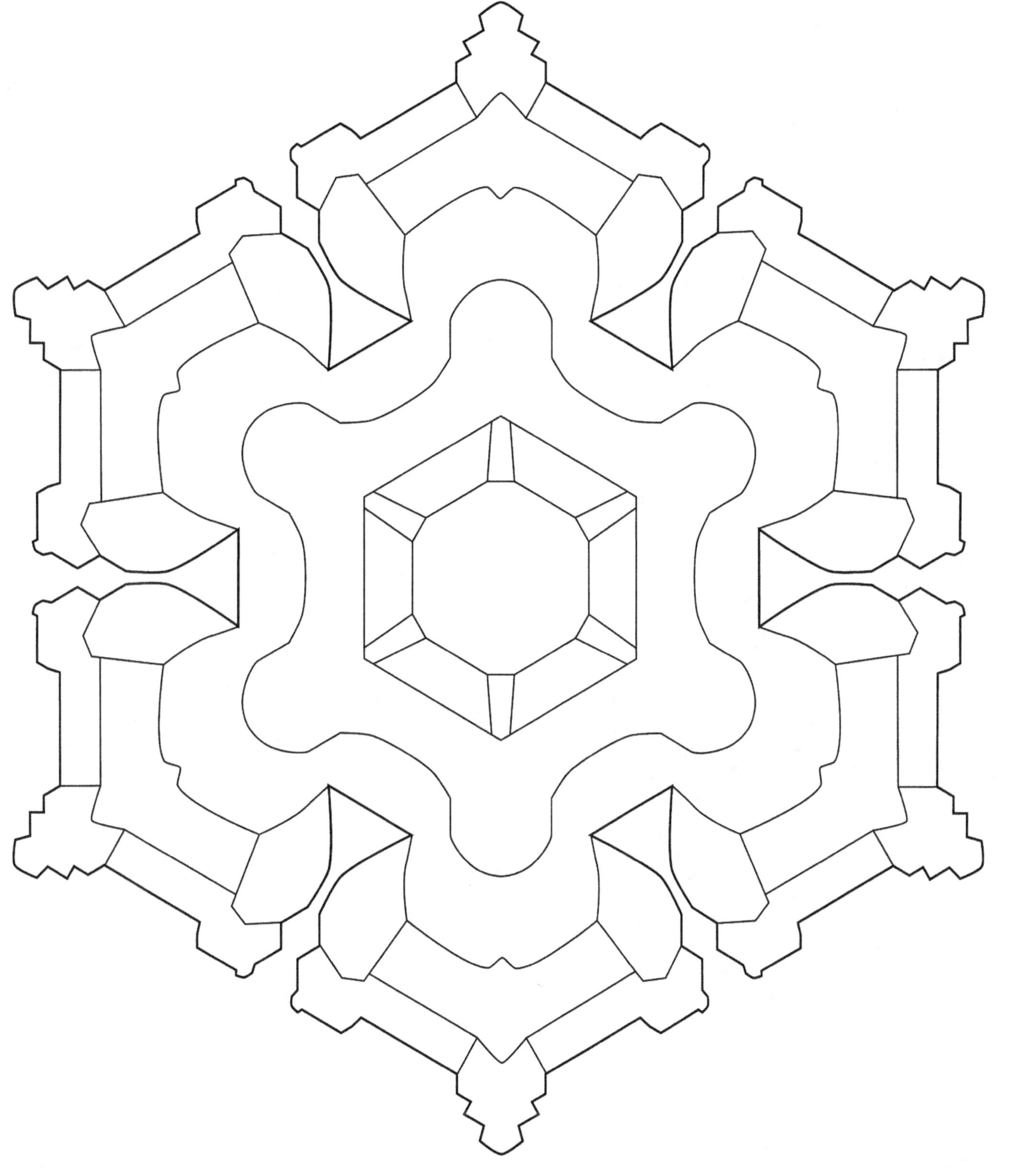

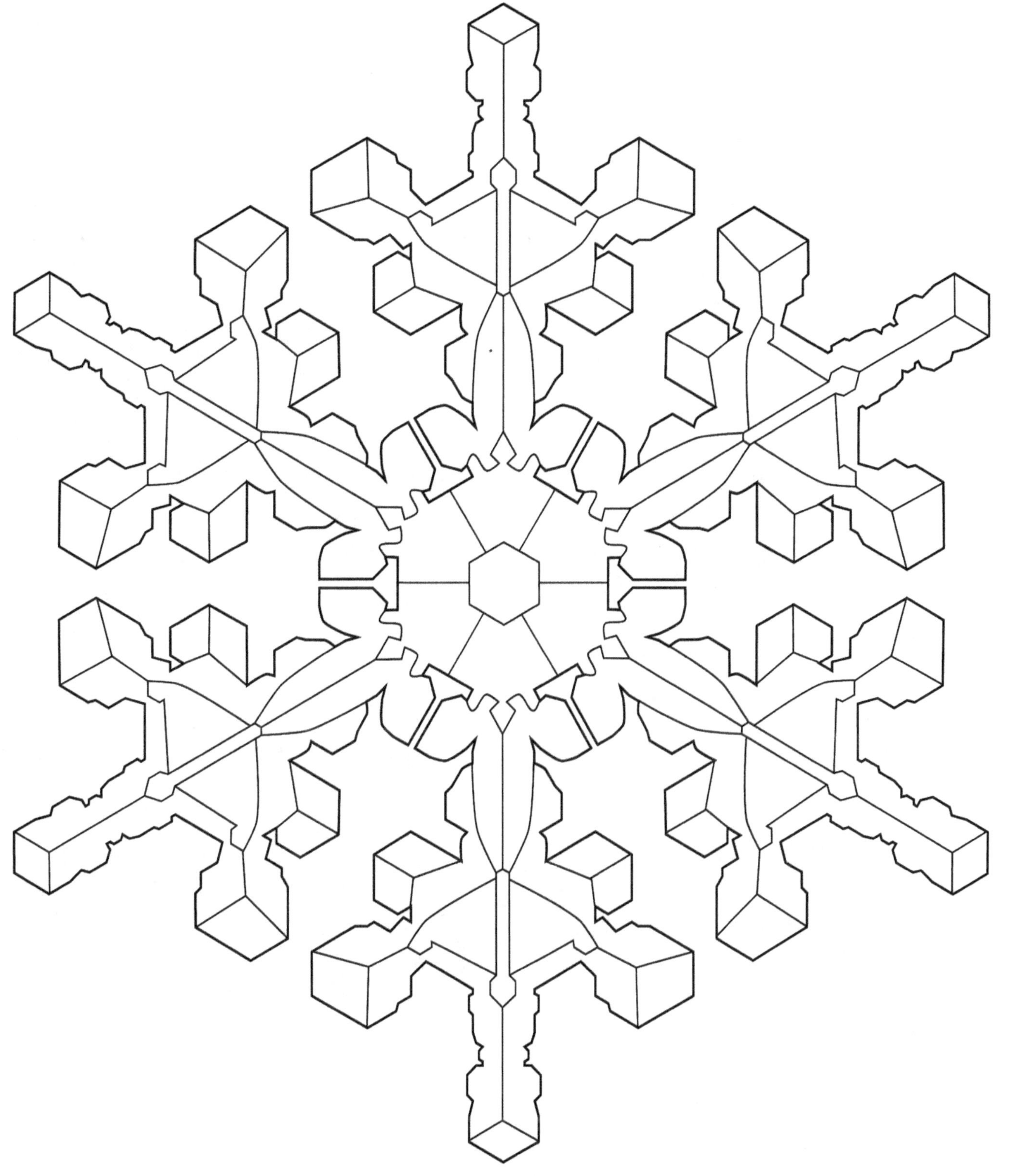

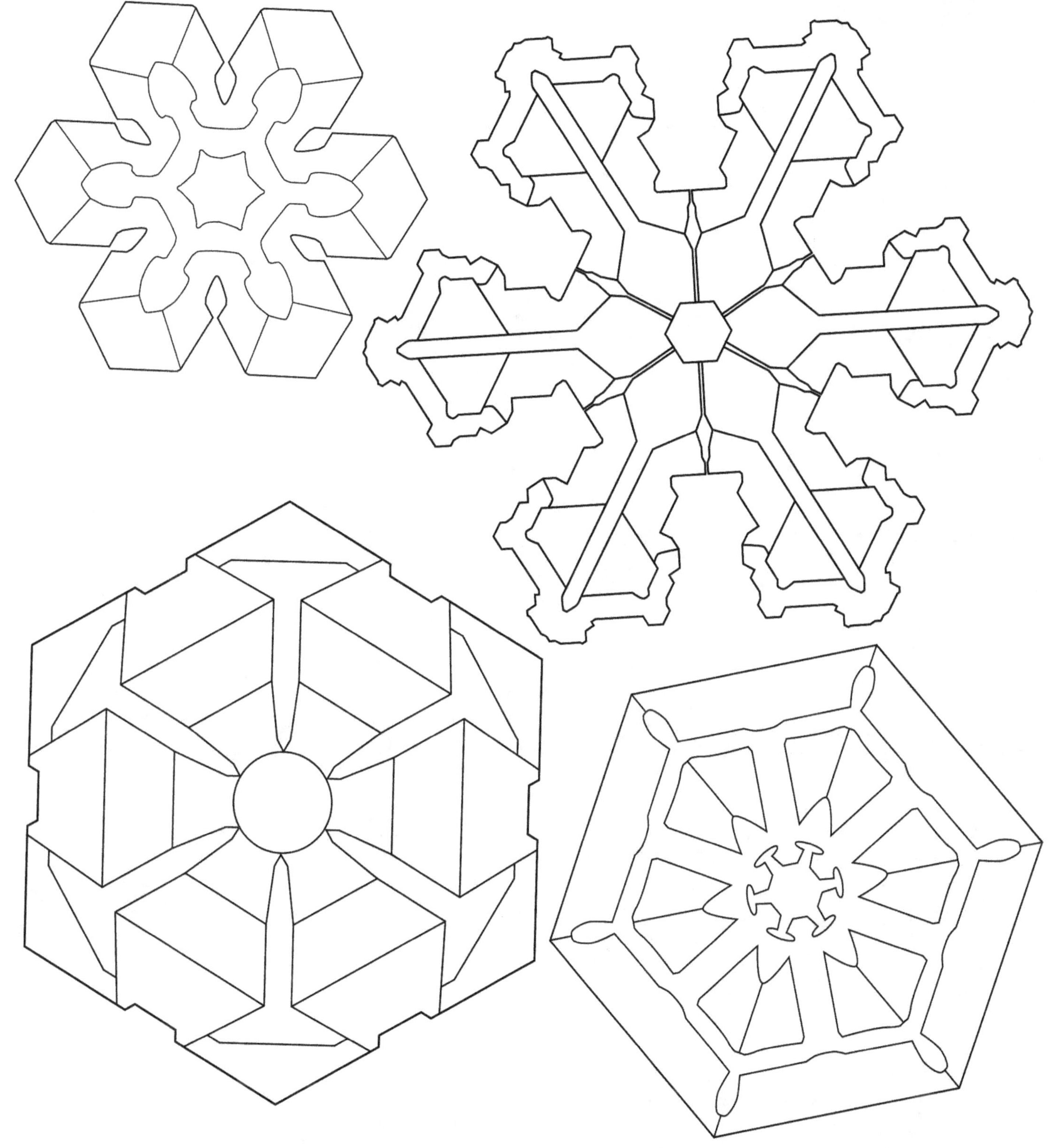

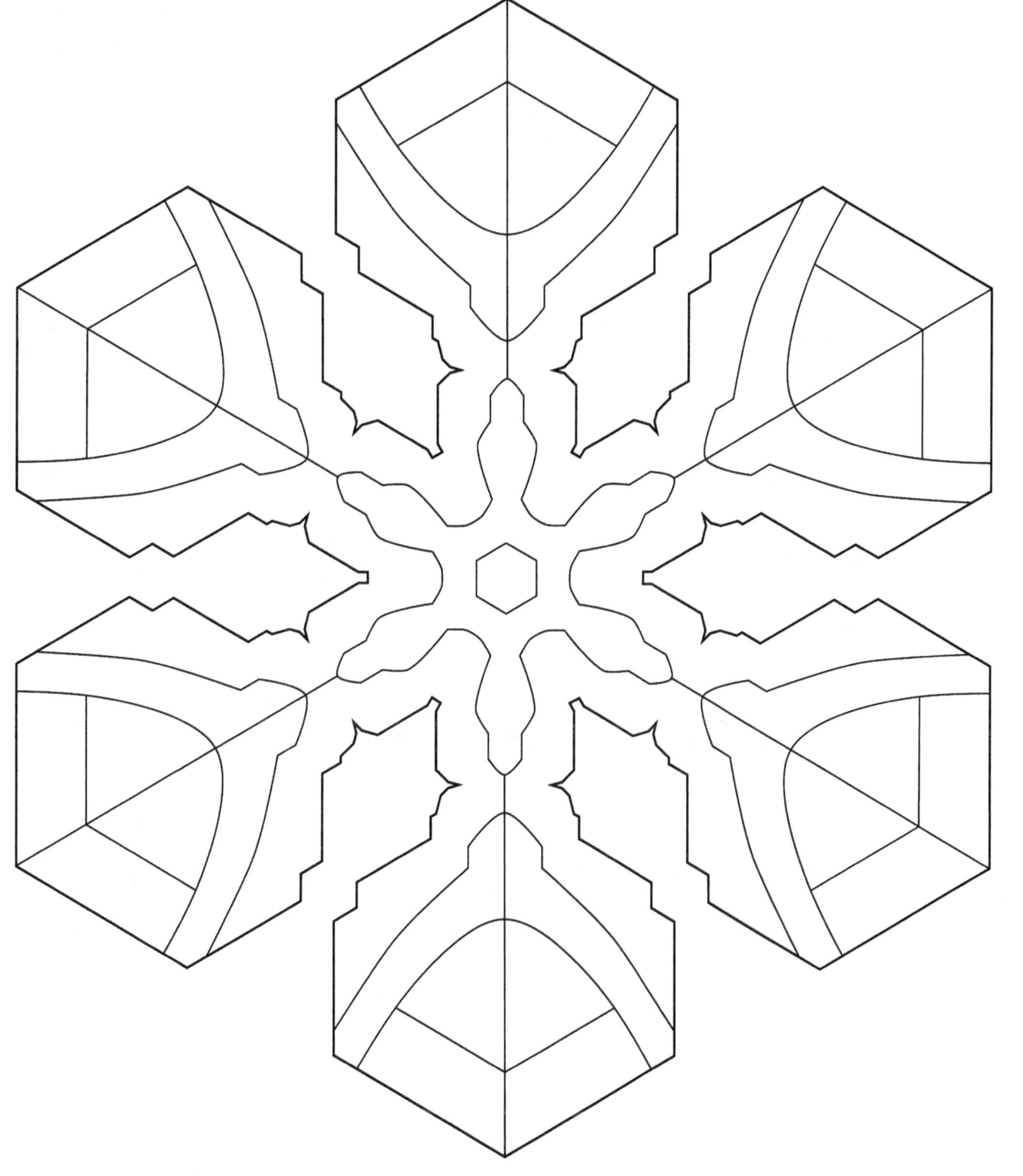

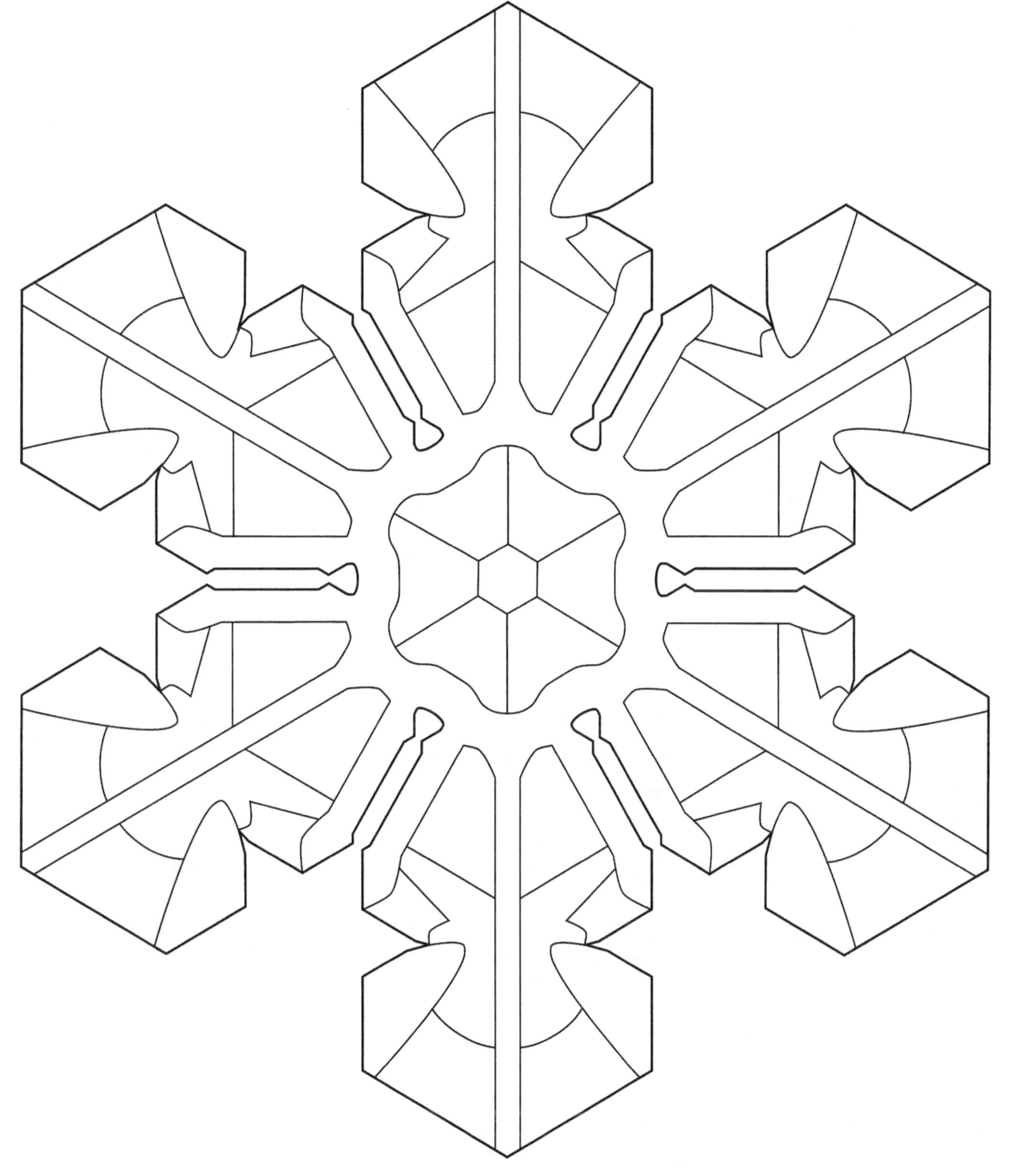

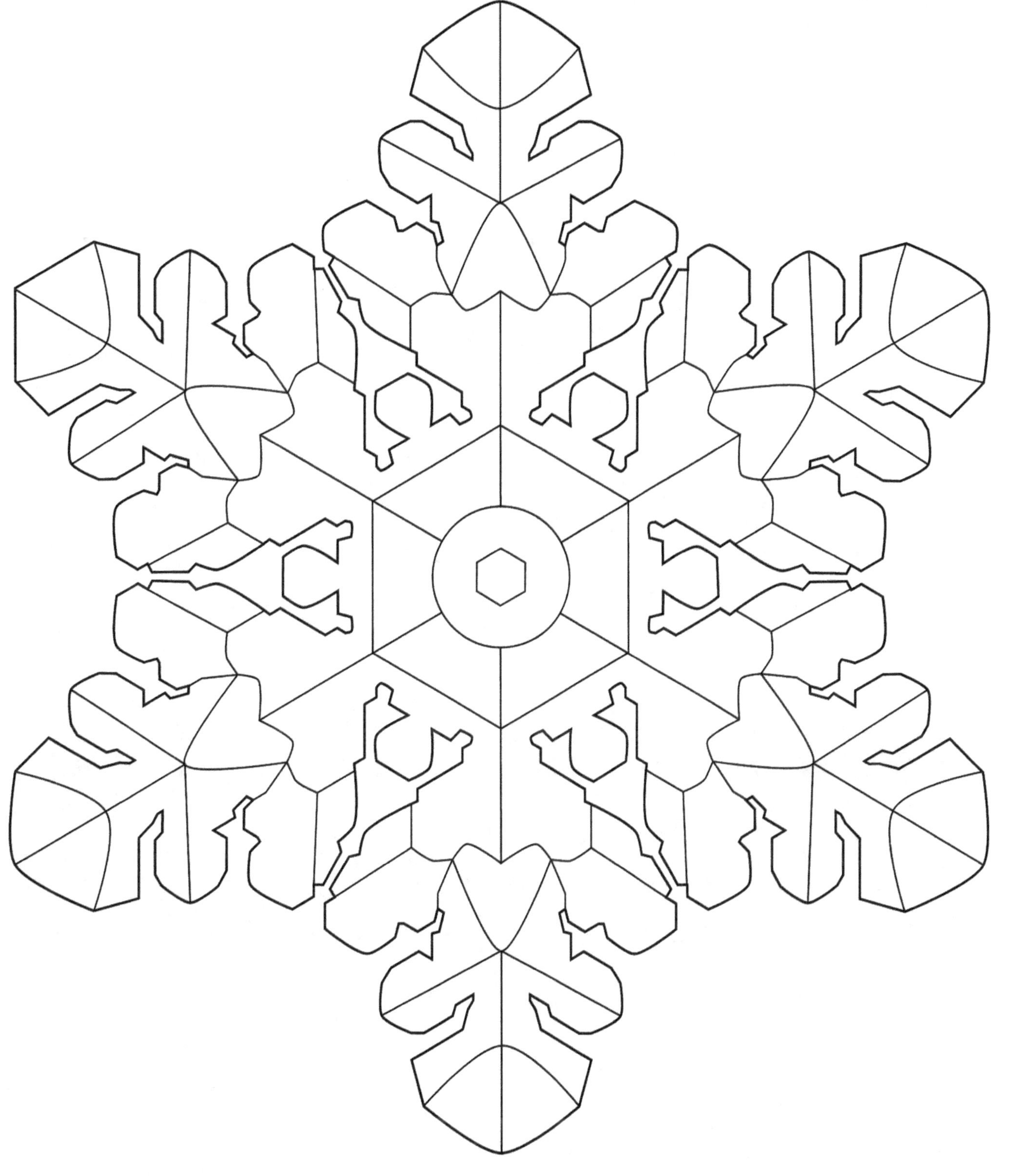

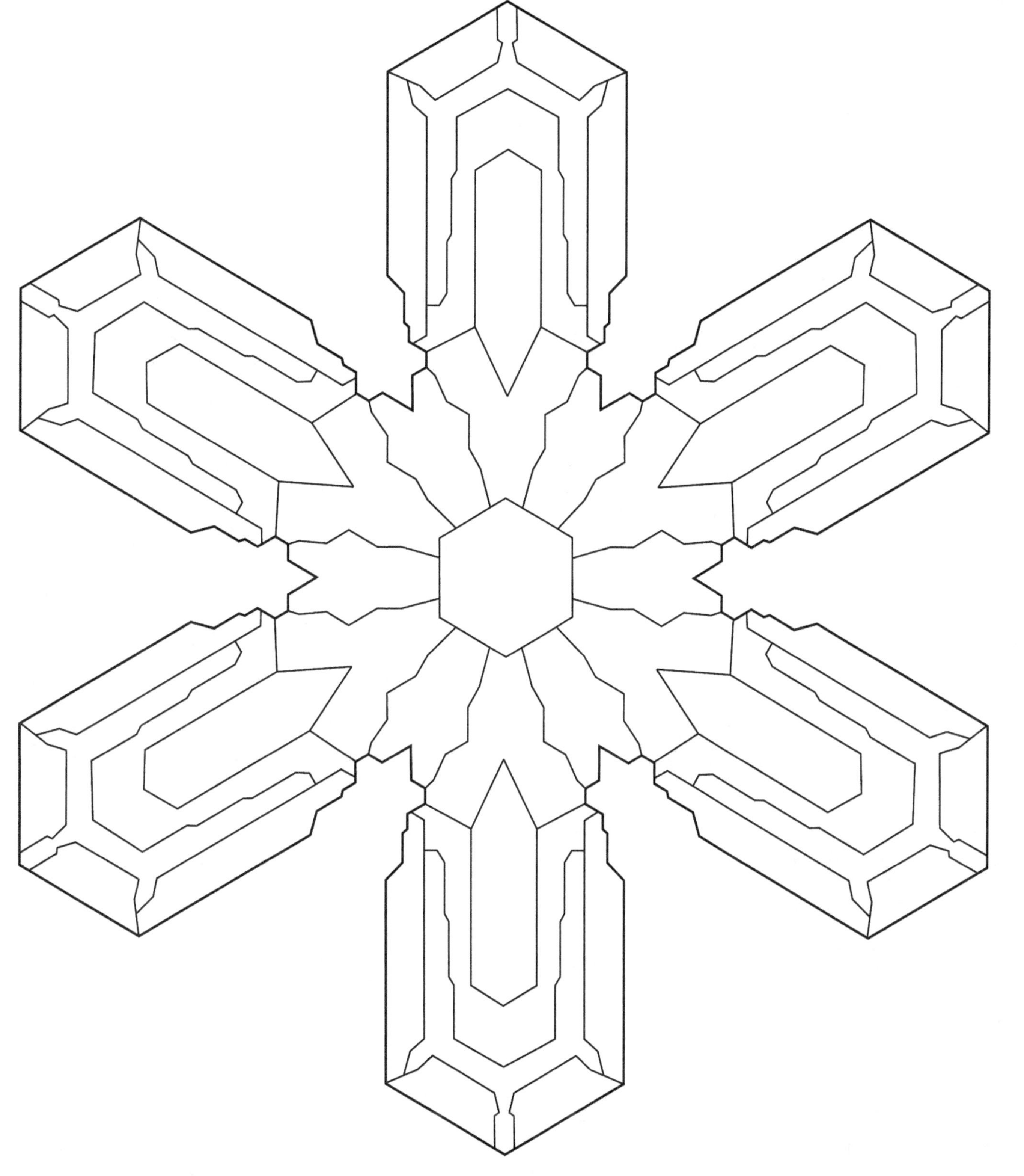

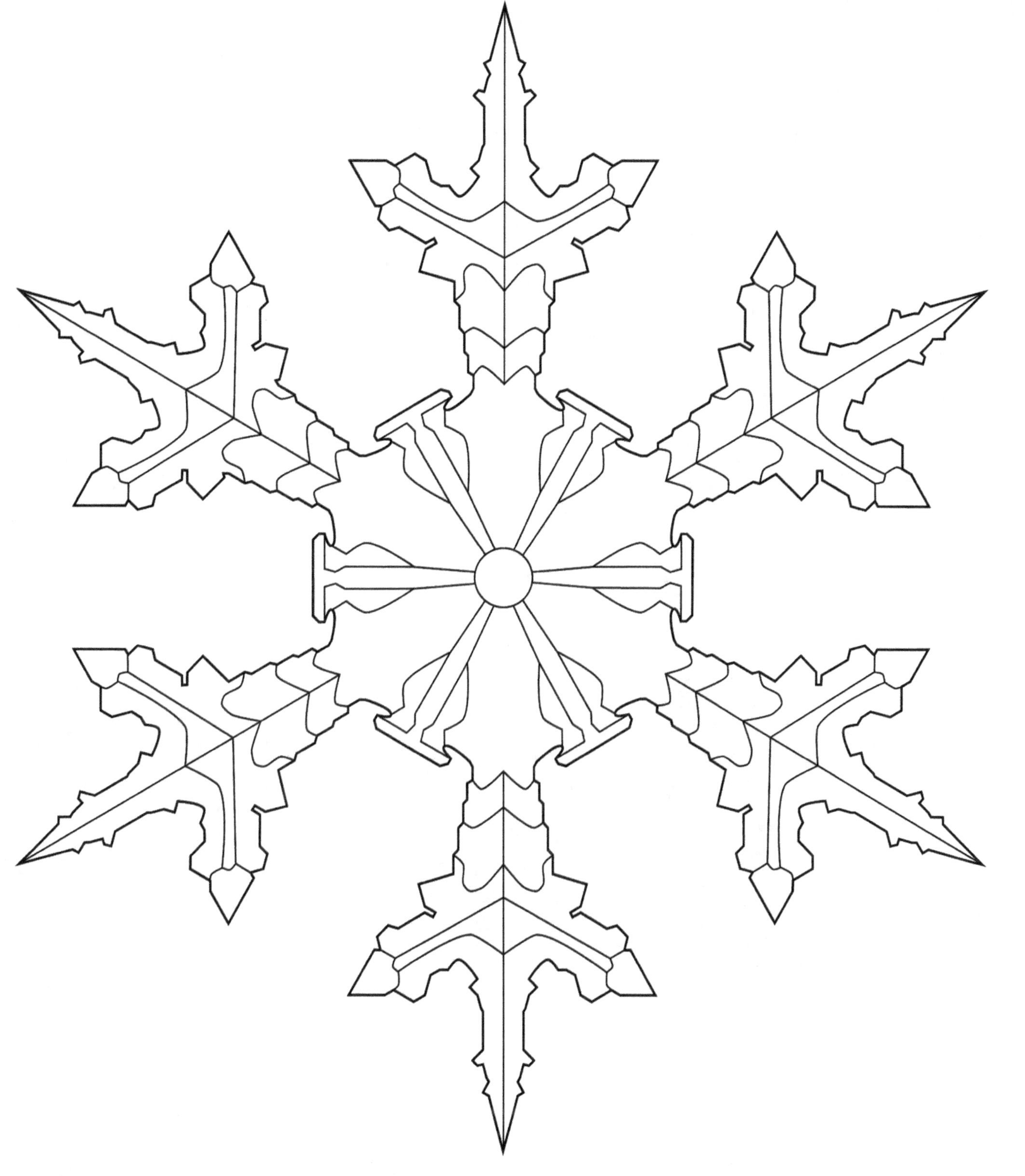

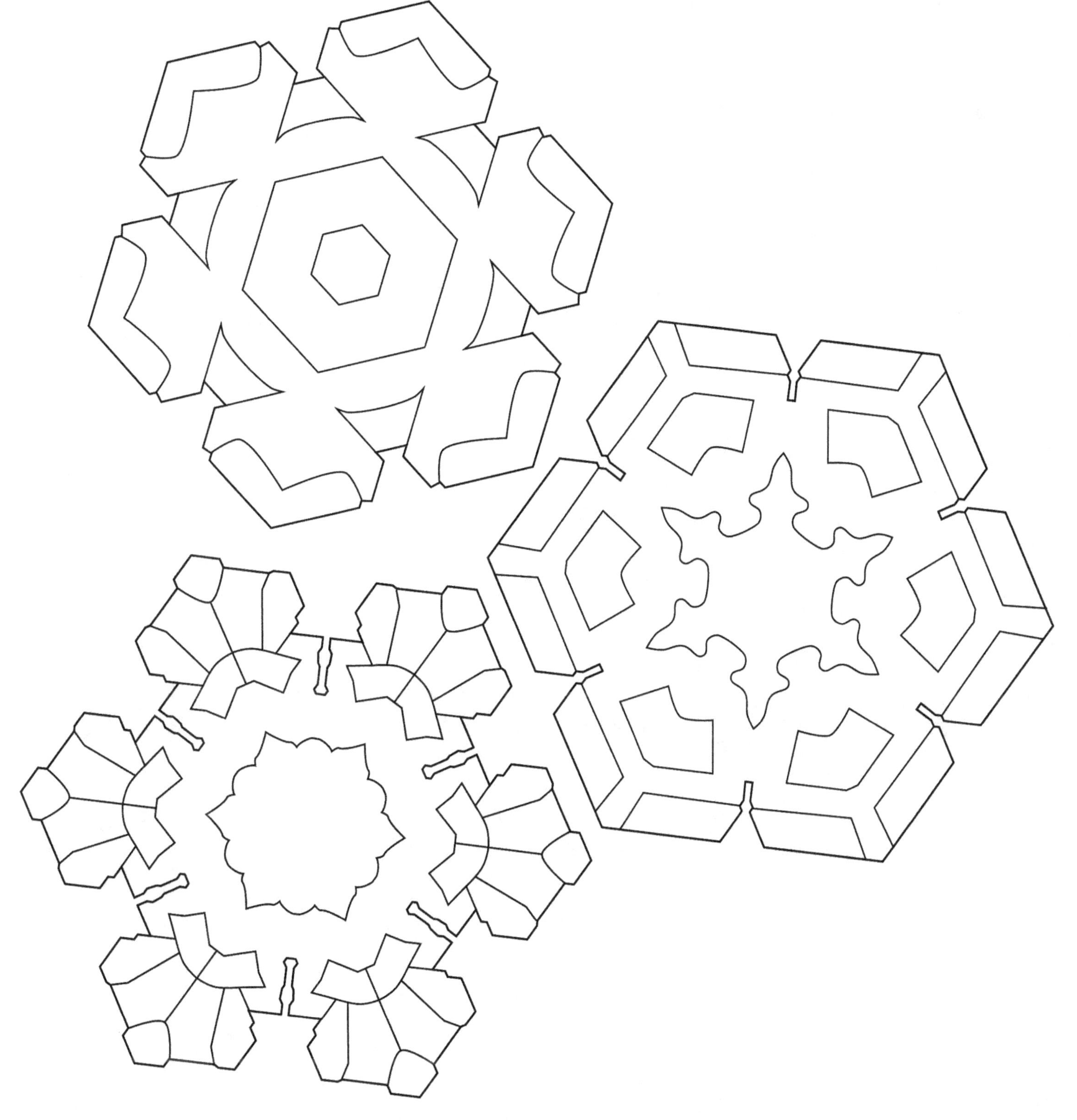

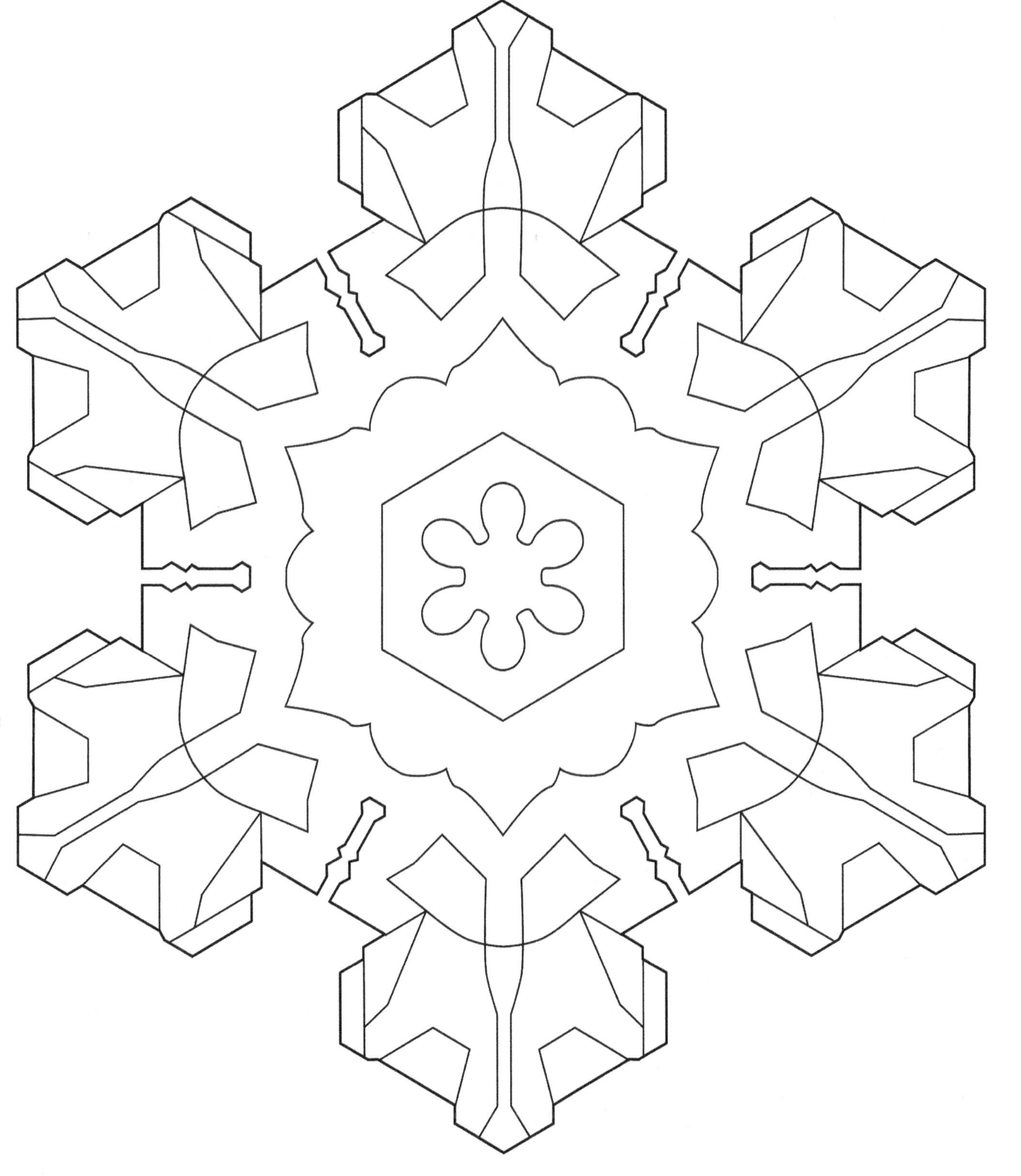

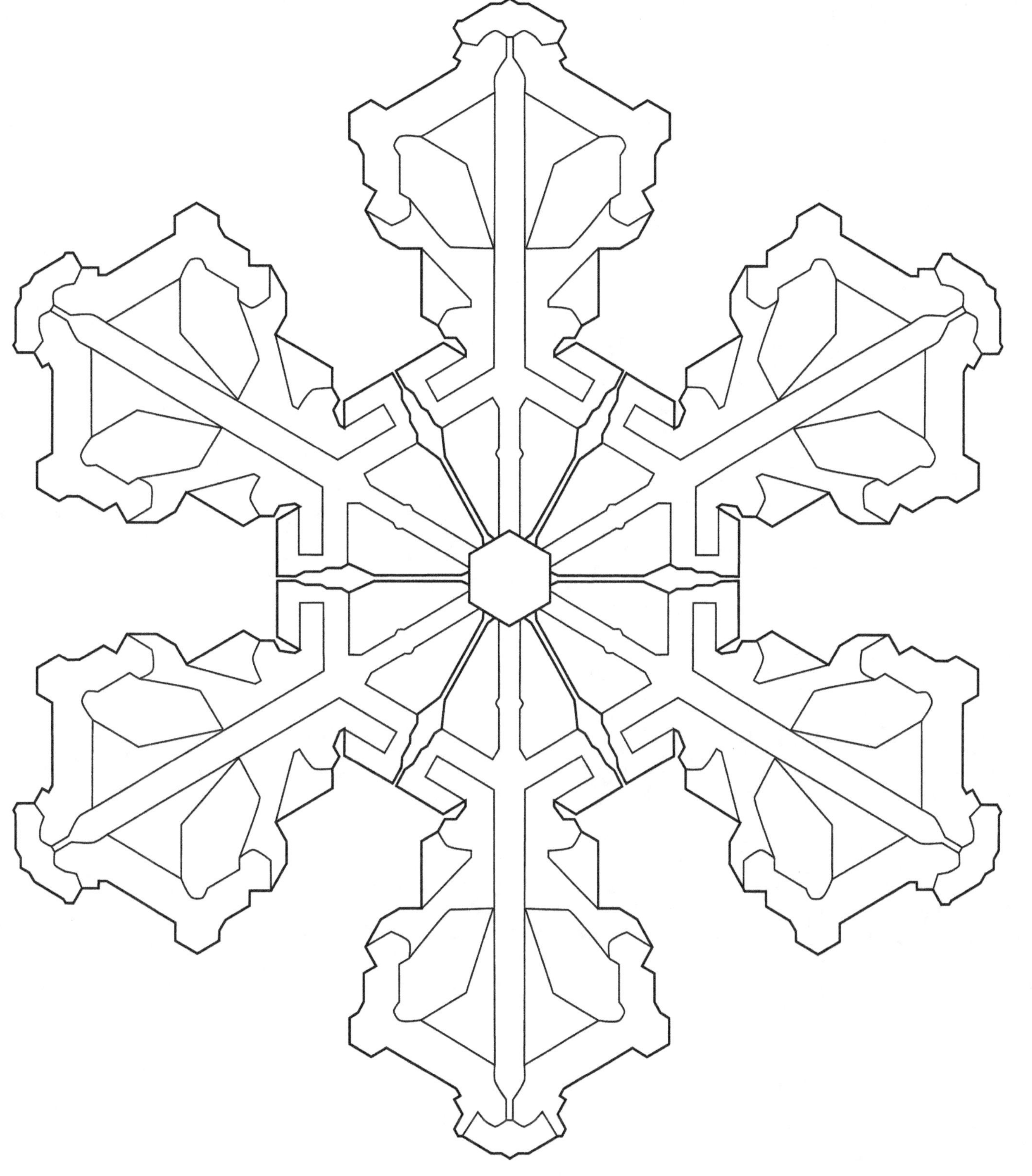

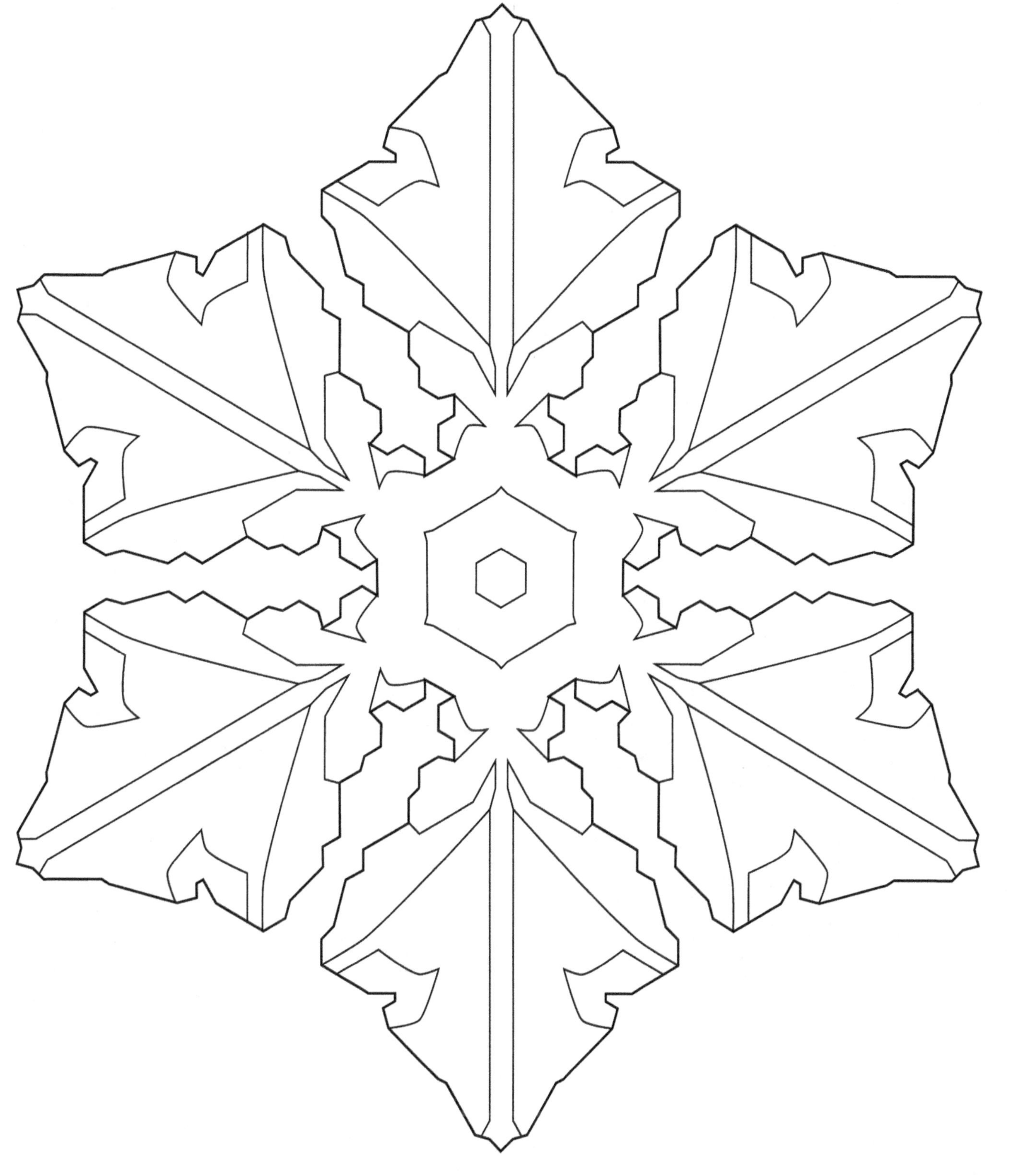

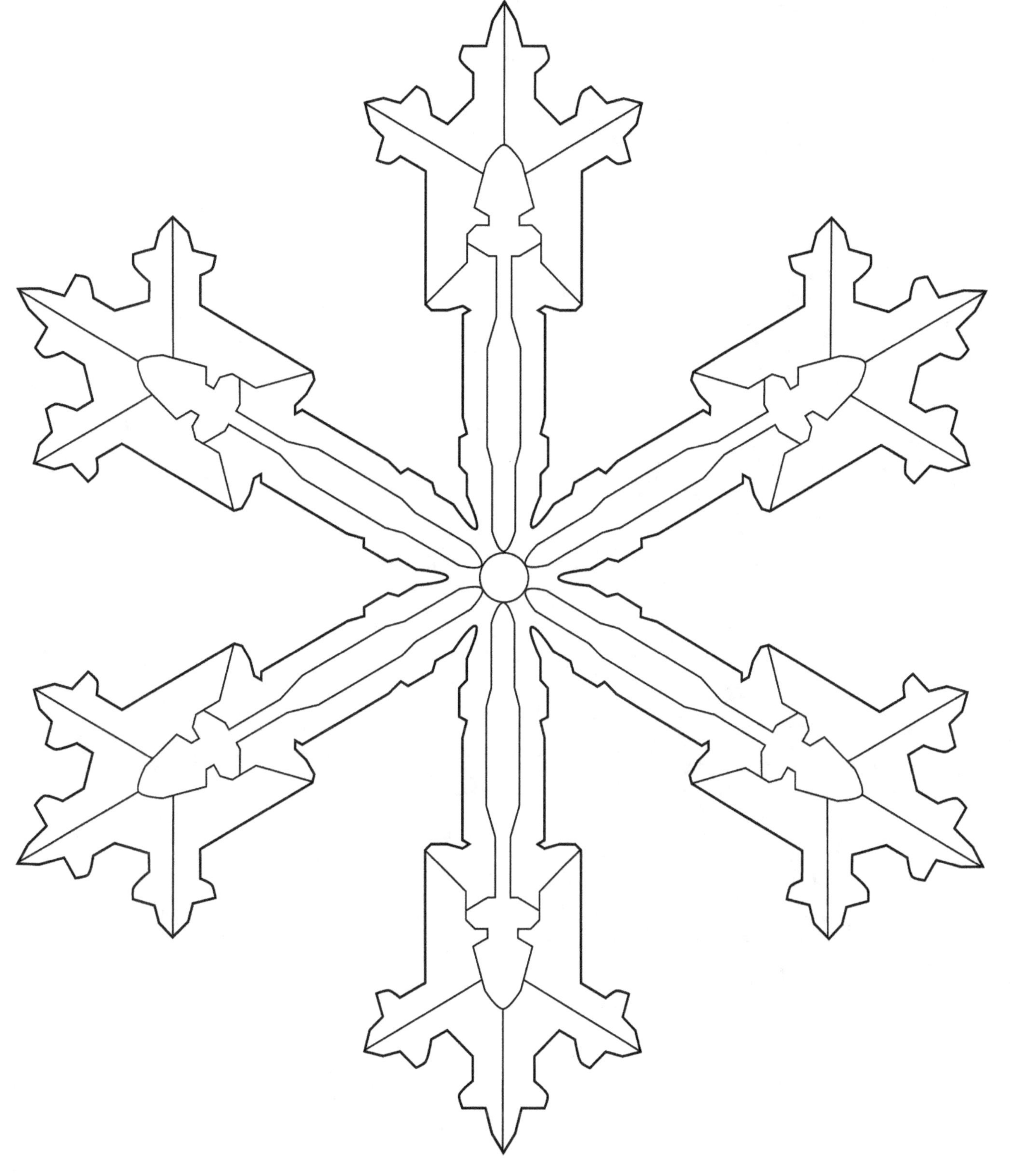

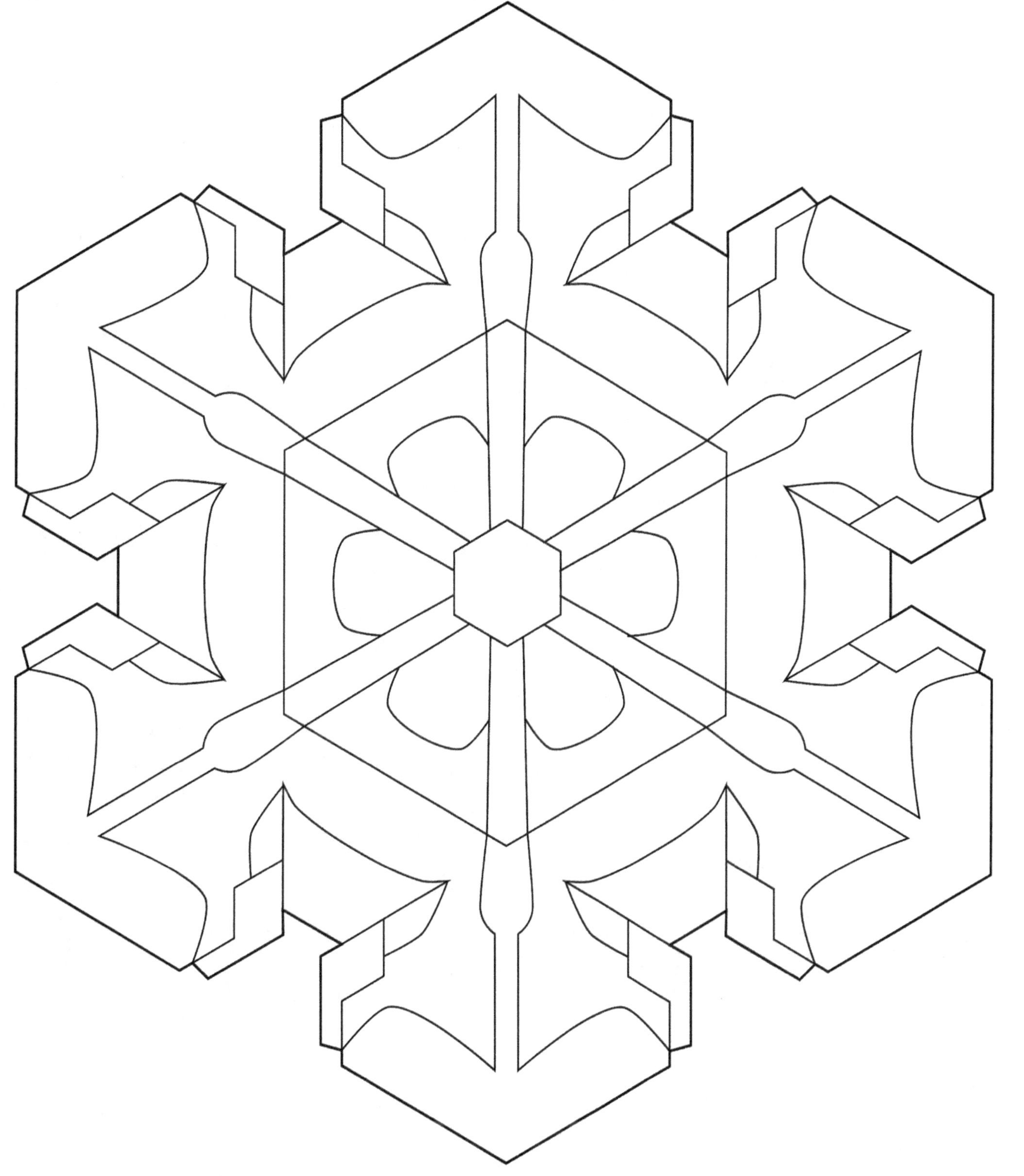

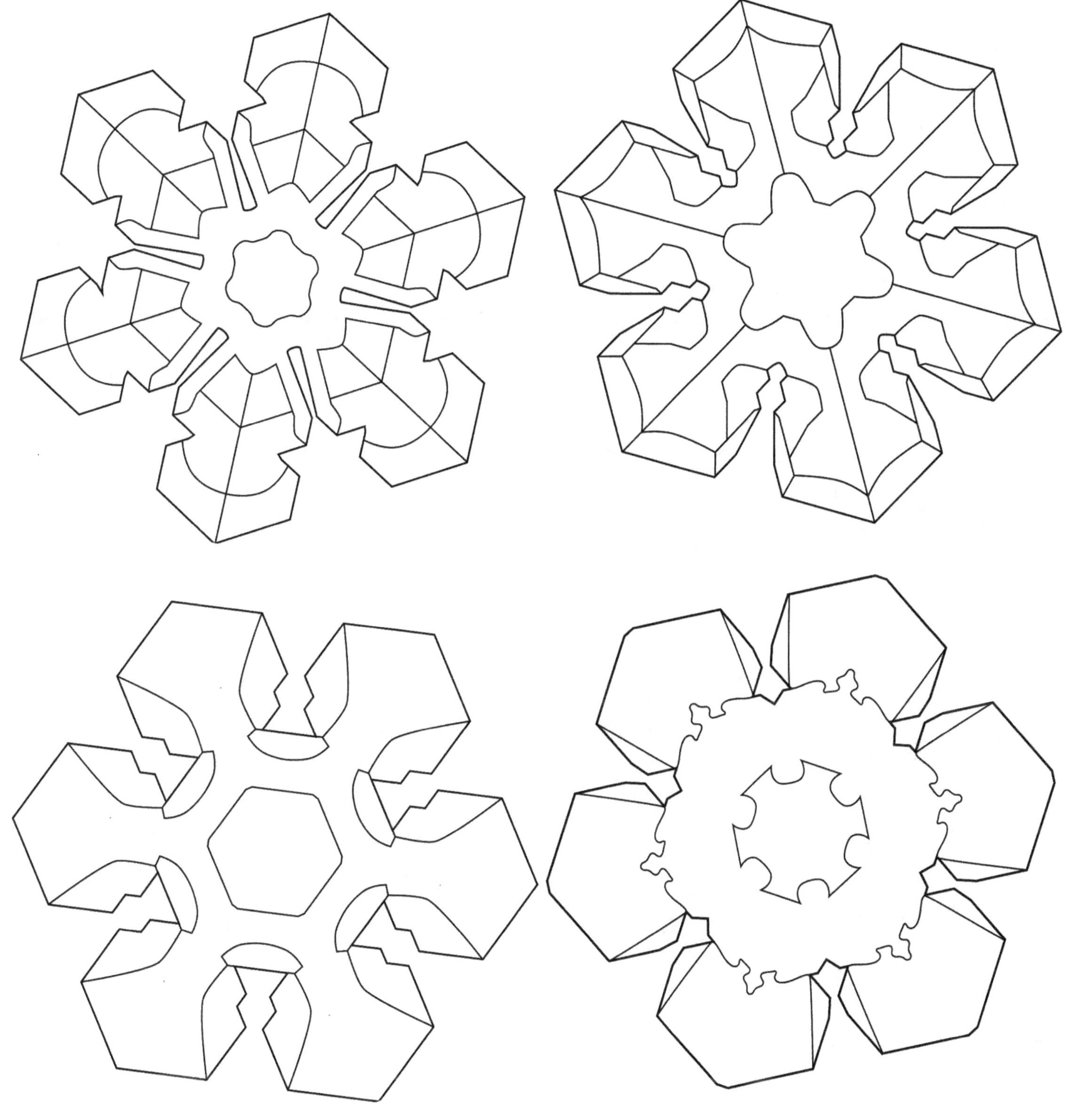

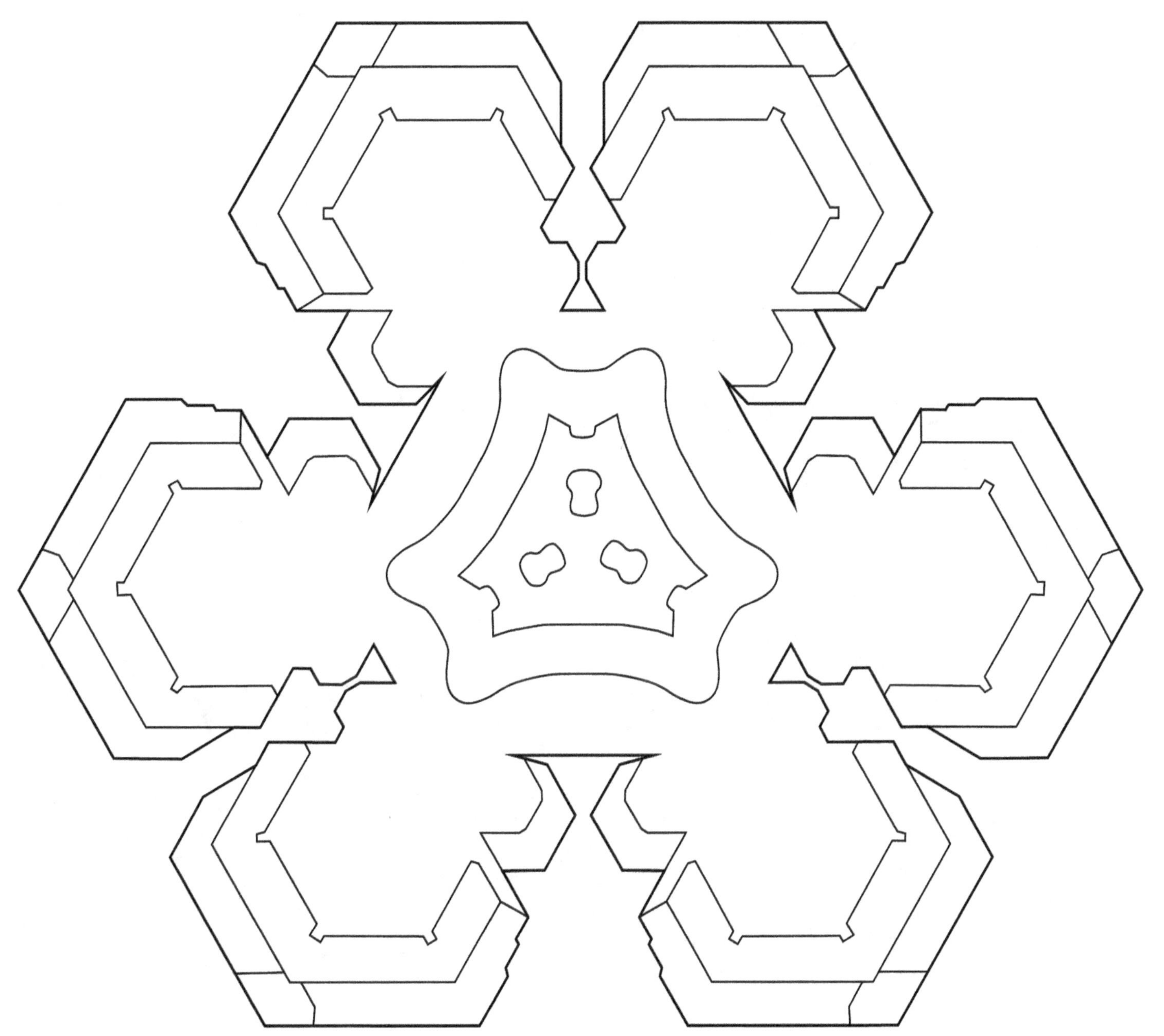

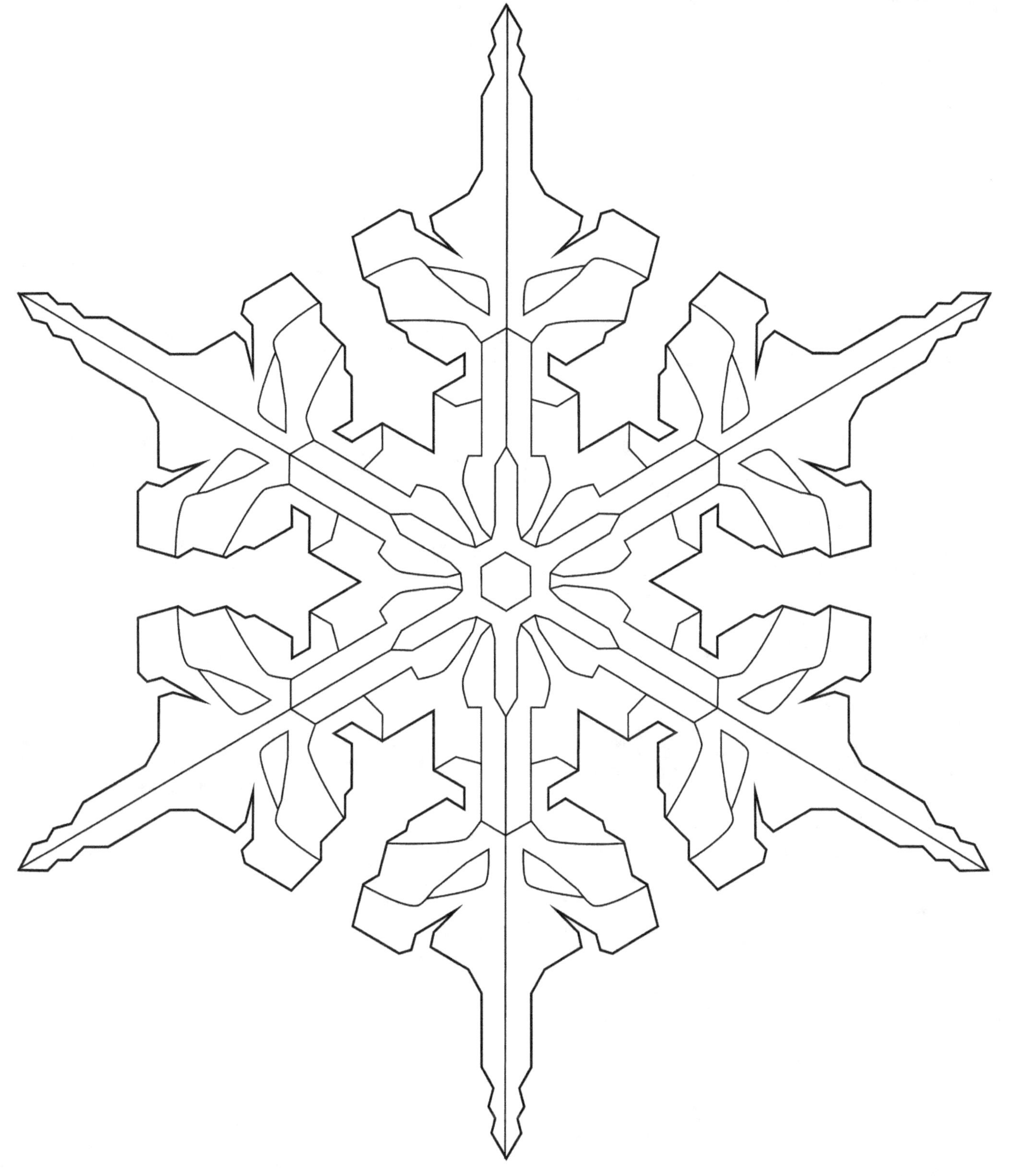

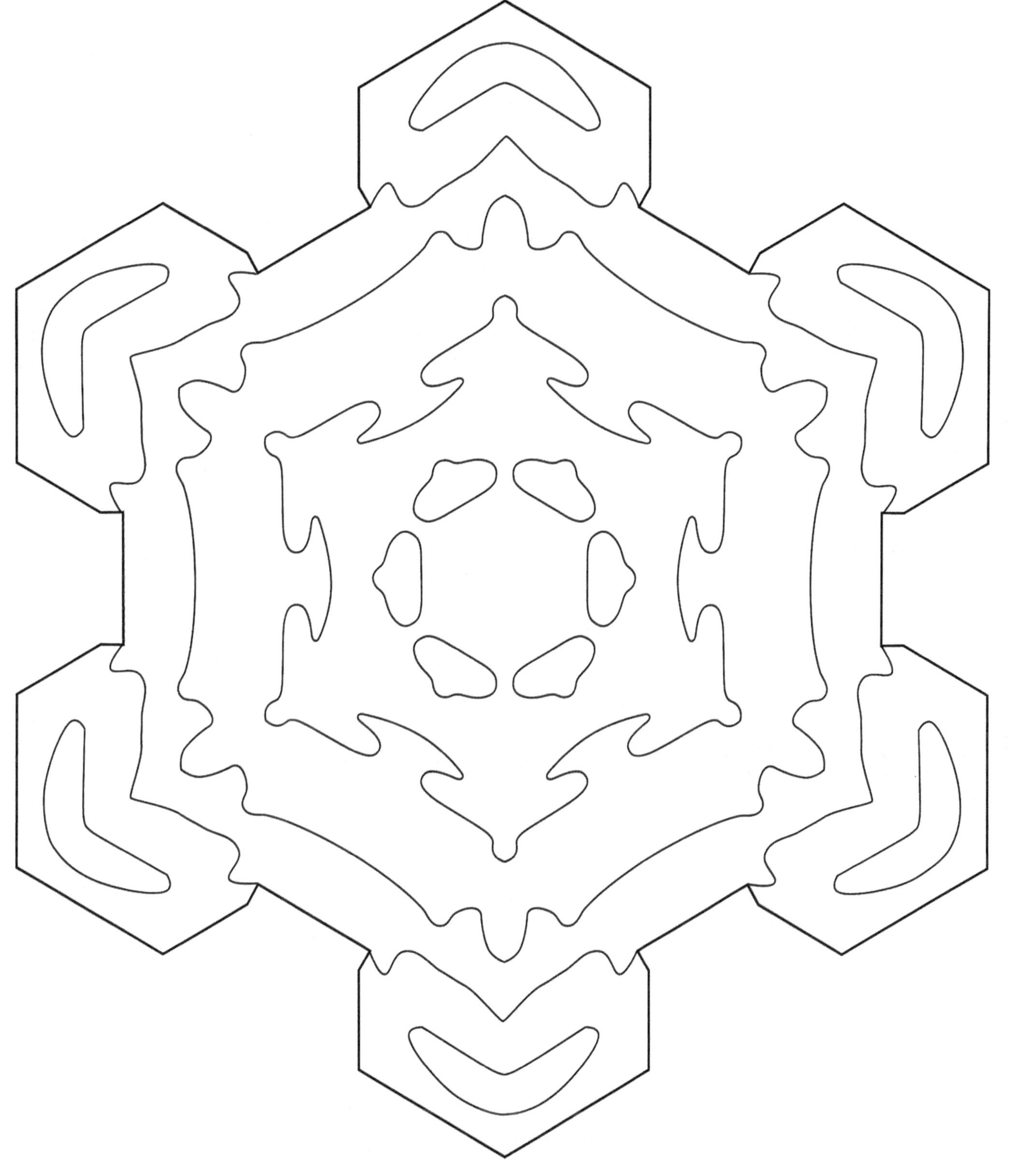

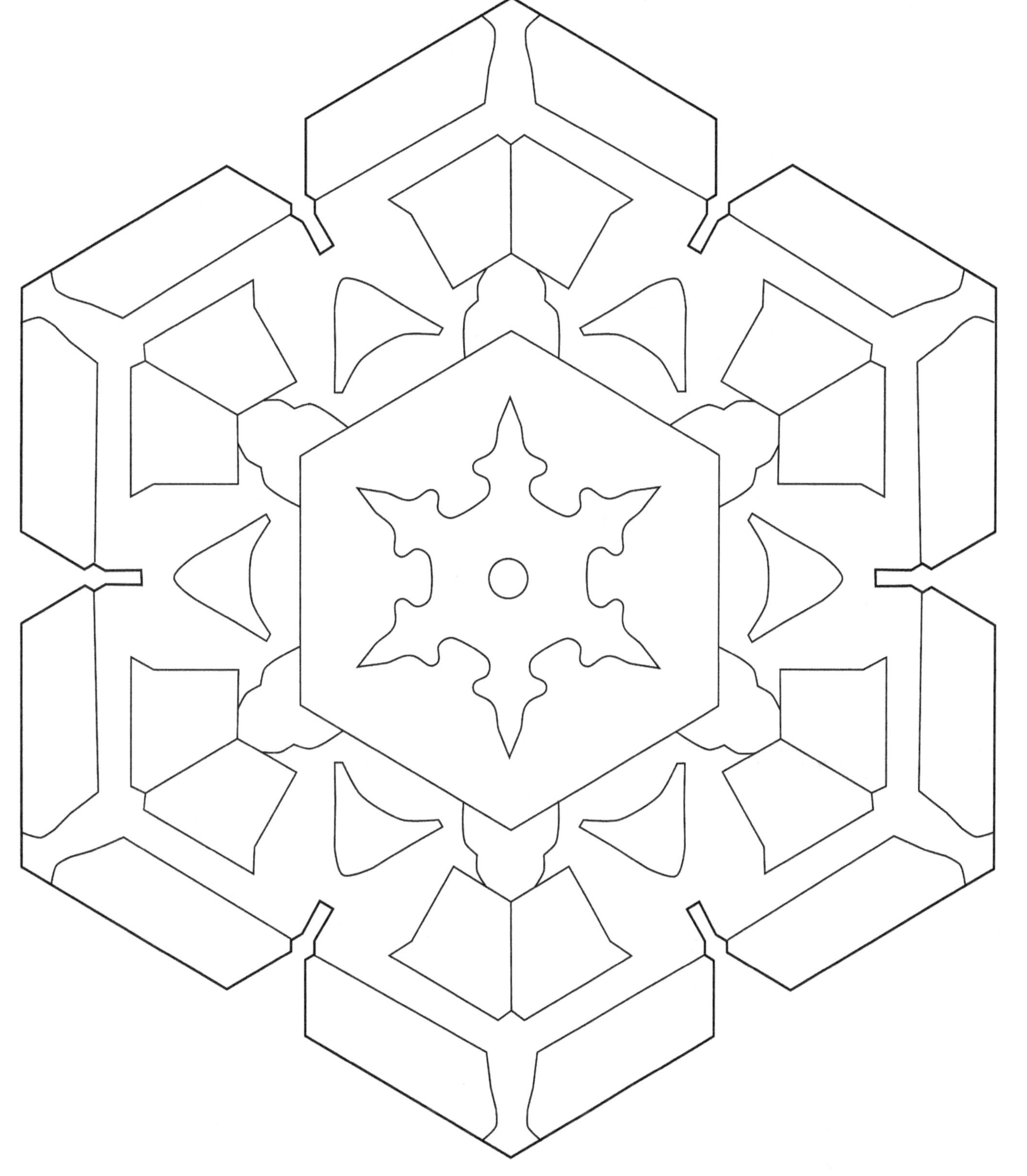

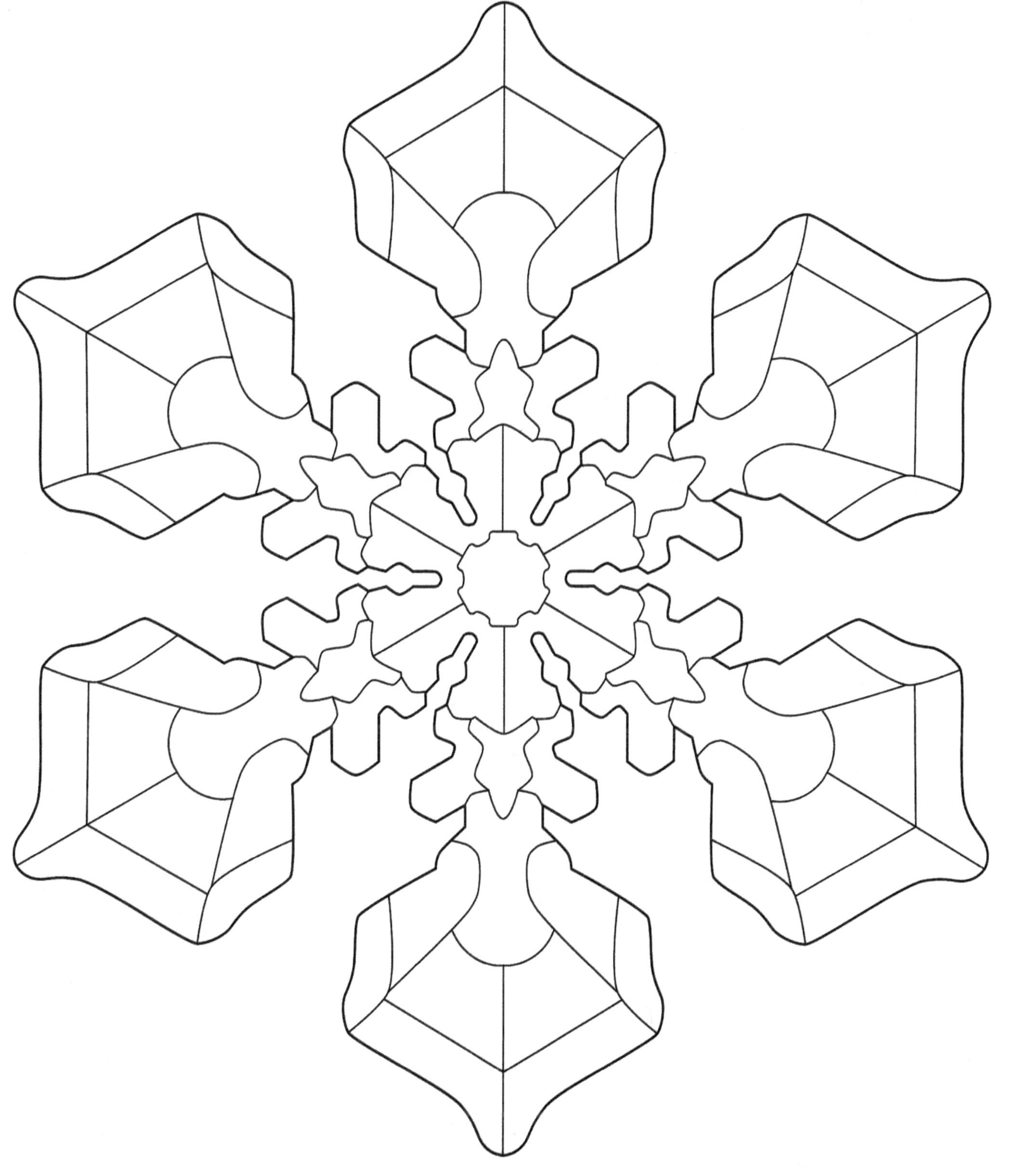

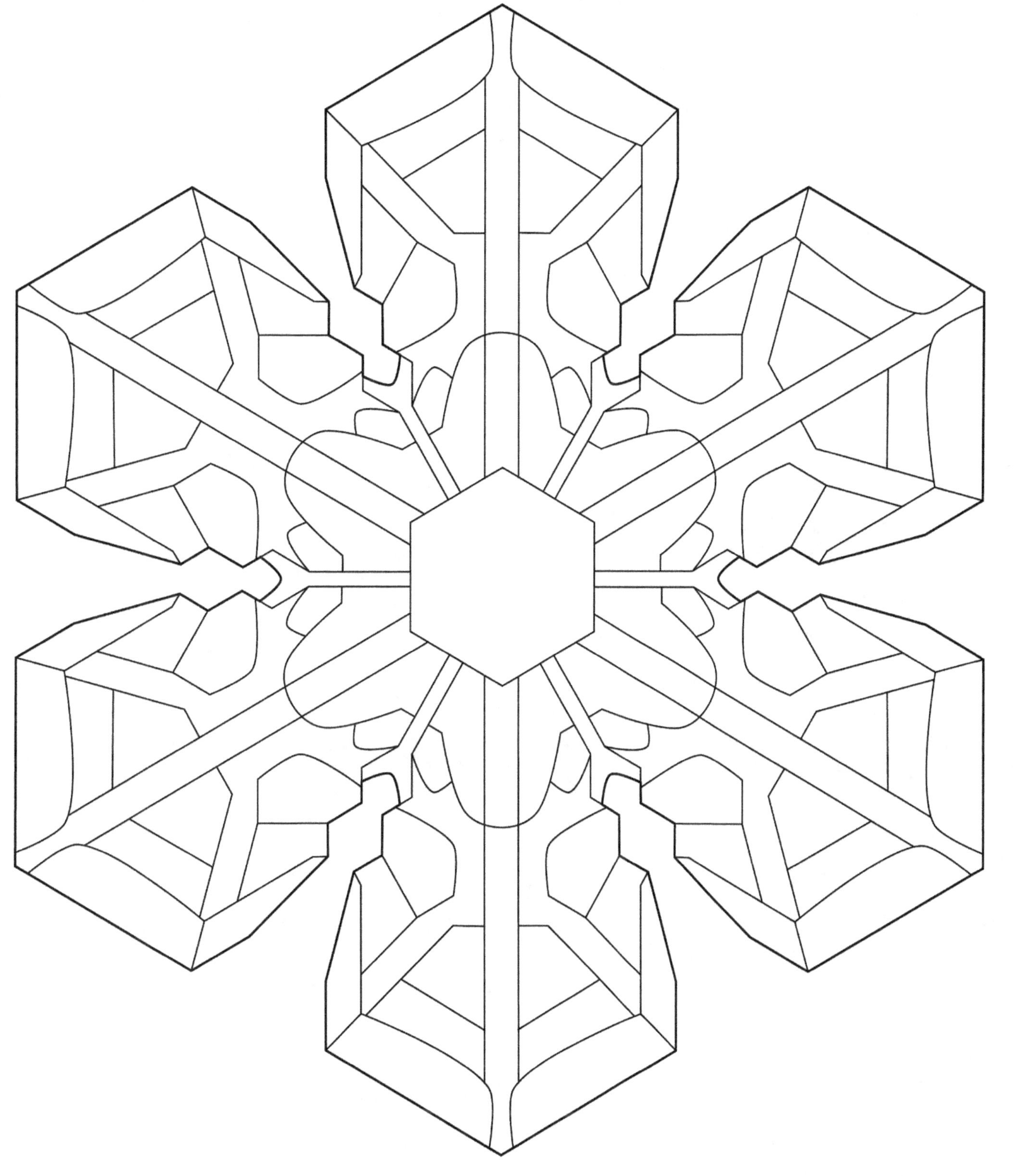

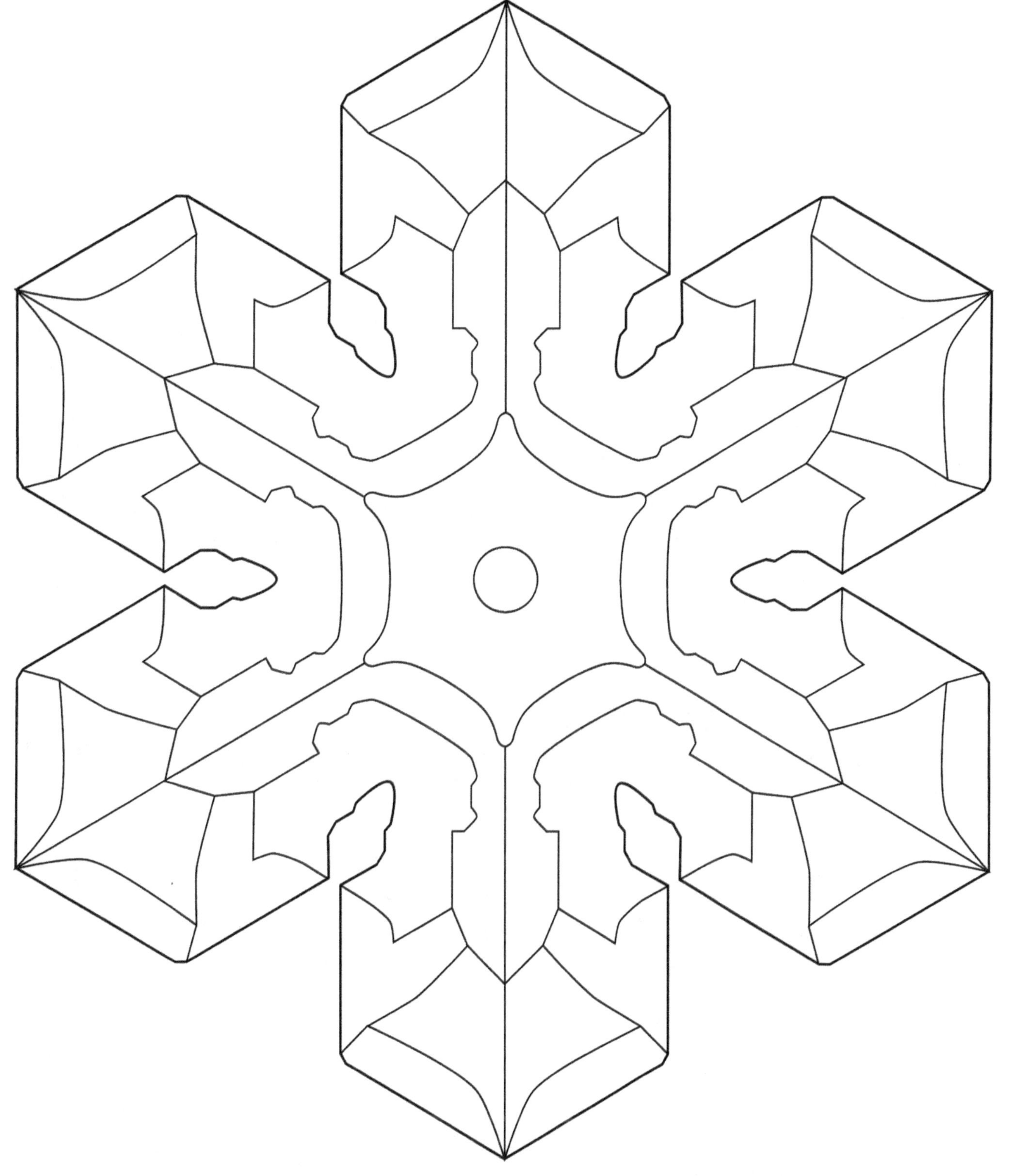

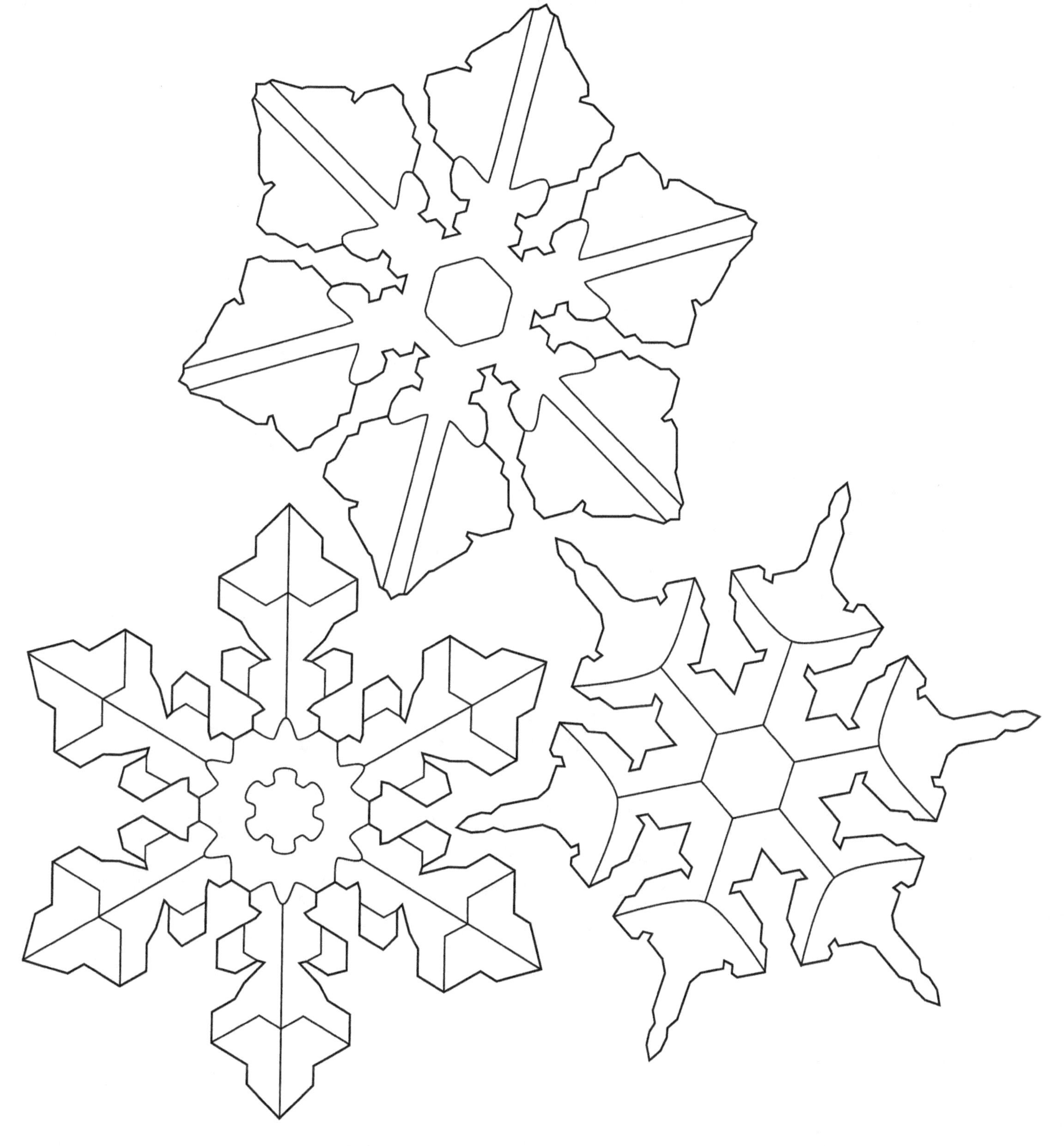

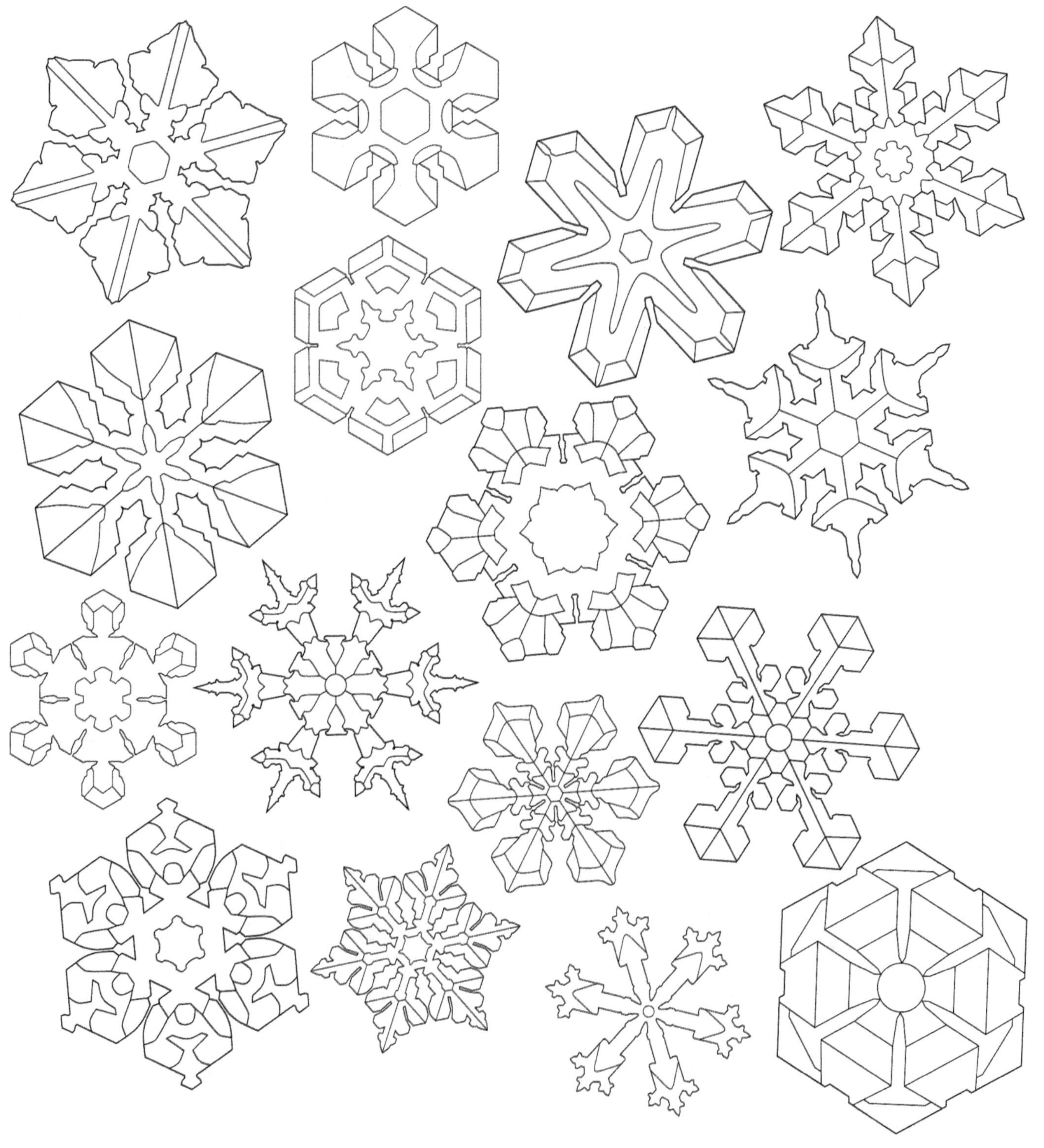

List of Snowflakes

Want to see the real photographs that inspired these drawings?
Go to www.FacetedPress.com/snowflakes and click on the flake.

Listed below are the flakes and their corresponding number on the website:

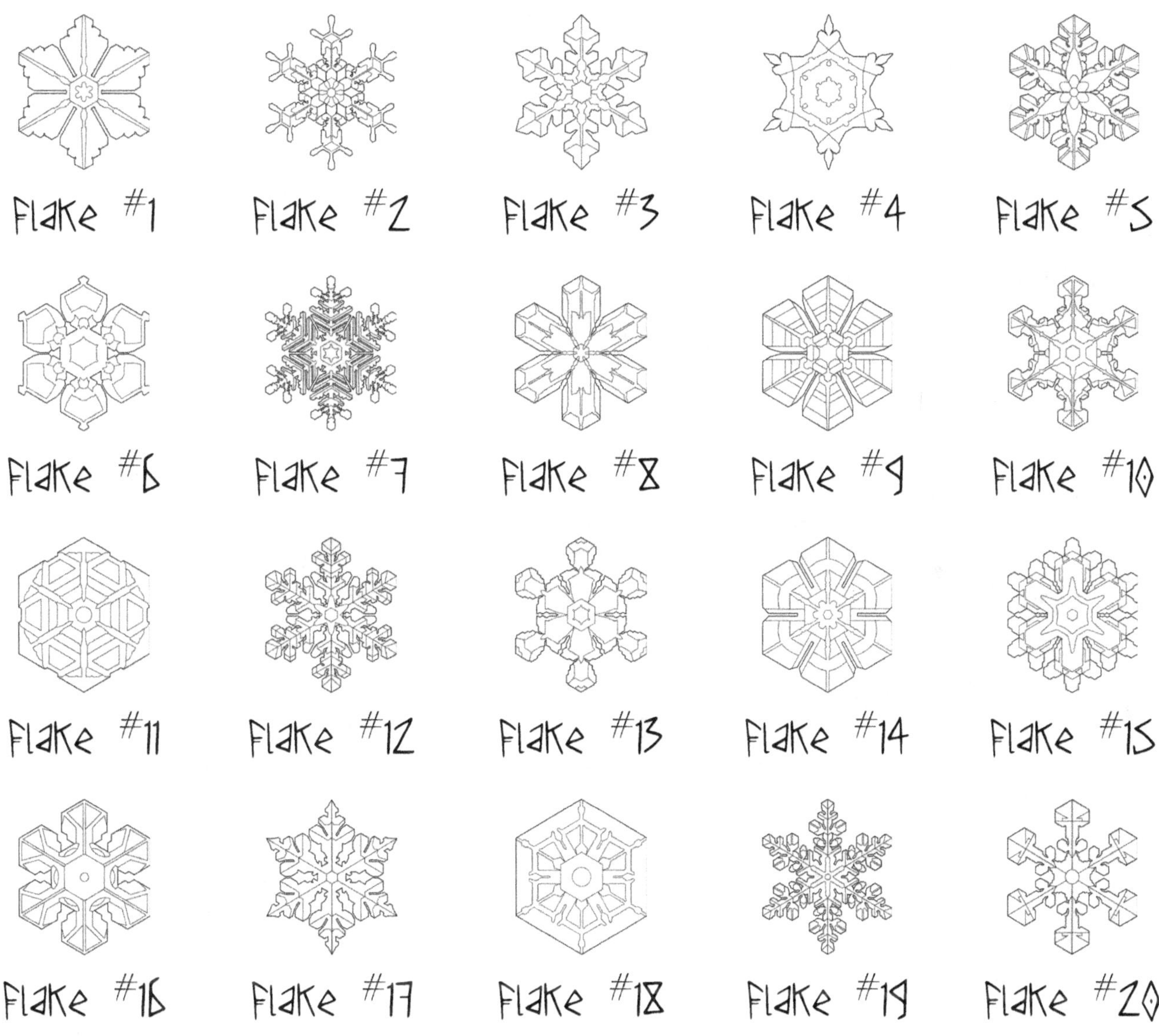

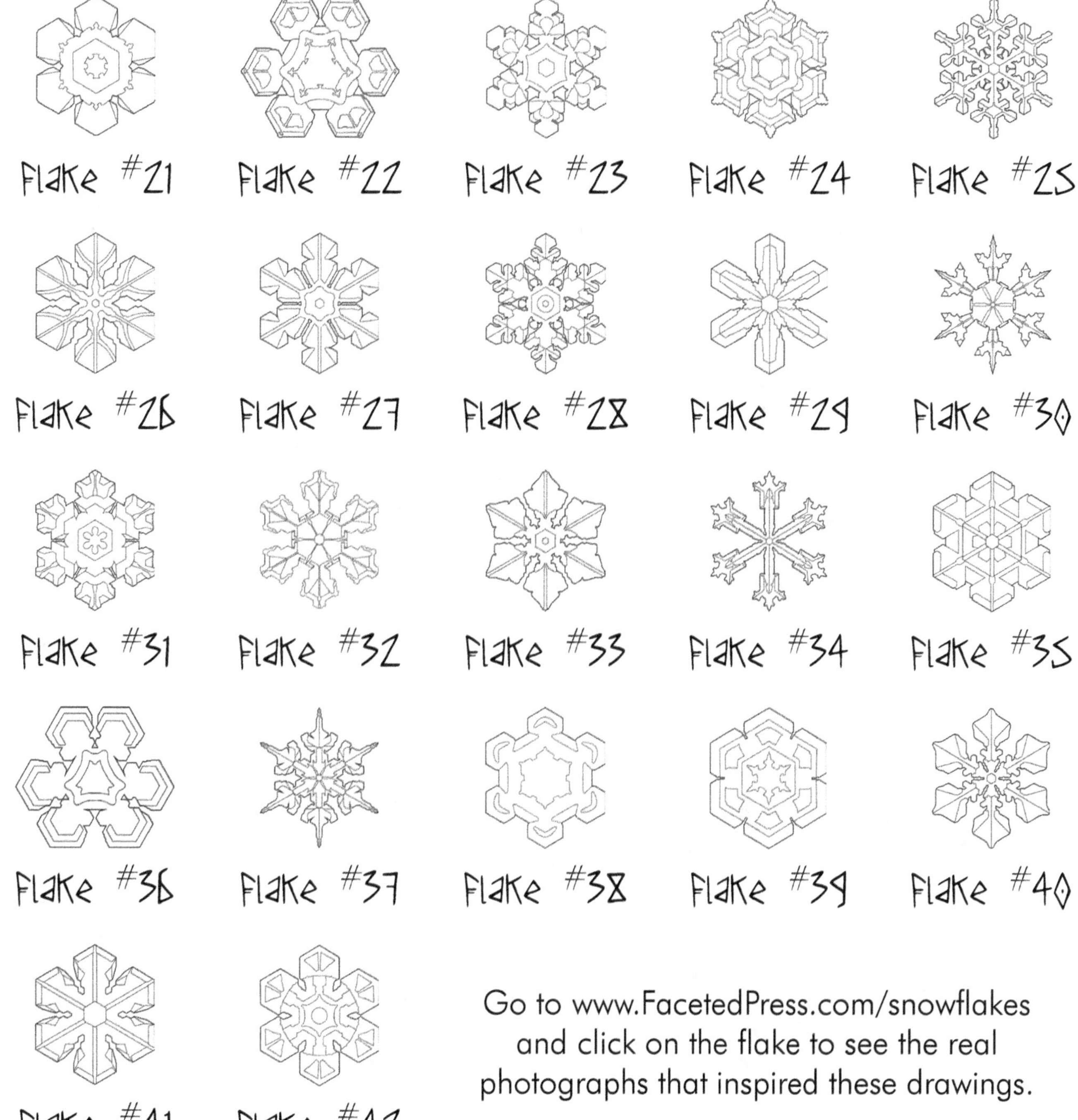

Go to www.FacetedPress.com/snowflakes
and click on the flake to see the real
photographs that inspired these drawings.